VICTORIA'S
MOST HAUNTED

D1510028

DISCARDED

DISCARDED

VICTORIA'S
MOST HAUNTED

Ghost Stories from BC's
Historic Capital City

IAN GIBBS

TOUCHWOOD
EDITIONS

3 1357 00314 2293

Copyright © 2017 by Ian Gibbs

All rights reserved. No part of this publication may be reproduced, stored in a retrieval system, or transmitted in any form or by any means, electronic, mechanical, photocopying, recording, or otherwise, without the prior written permission of the publisher. For more information, contact the publisher:

TouchWood Editions
103–1075 Pendergast Street
Victoria, BC V8V 0A1
Touchwoodeditions.com

The information in this book is true and complete to the best of the author's knowledge. All recommendations are made without guarantee on the part of the author or the publisher.

Edited by Kate Scallion
Cover design by Pete Kohut
Interior design by Setareh Ashrafologhalai
Proofread by Claire Philipson
Photo credits on page 199

LIBRARY AND ARCHIVES CANADA CATALOGUING IN PUBLICATION
Gibbs, Ian, 1972–, author
     Victoria's most haunted : ghost stories from BC's historic capital city/Ian Gibbs.

Issued in print and electronic formats.
ISBN 978-1-77151-213-8 (softcover)

1. Ghosts—British Columbia—Victoria. 2. Haunted places—
     British Columbia—Victoria. I. Title.
     BF1472.C3G515 2017   133.109711'28   C2017-900366-6
     C2017-900367-4

We acknowledge the financial support of the Government of Canada through the Canada Book Fund and the Canada Council for the Arts, and of the province of British Columbia through the British Columbia Arts Council and the Book Publishing Tax Credit.

The interior pages of this book have been printed on 100% post-consumer recycled paper, processed chlorine free, and printed with vegetable-based inks.

Printed in Canada at Friesens
21 20 19 18   2 3 4 5

For those who believe, but fear
For those who don't believe, but want to
For those who aren't sure, but love stories:
This book is for you.

The boundaries which divide life from death are at best shadowy and vague. Who shall say where the one ends, and where the other begins?

EDGAR ALLAN POE "The Premature Burial," first published in the *Philadelphia Dollar Newspaper*, 1844

CONTENTS

● OUTSIDE OF TOWN

FOREWORD

VICTORIA IS THE MOST haunted city in the Pacific Northwest, and local residents aren't shy about letting everyone know it. In North America, half the population believes in ghosts; the other half don't—or at least they don't want to admit they do. In Victoria, however, the proportion of believers is well above fifty percent. Those of us who actively collect and tell ghost stories soon discover that wherever we go people single us out to recount their personal encounters with ghosts, or to express a real curiosity about the spirit world. Fully twenty percent of Canadians have had a documented experience with a ghost, but it seems in Victoria there's a higher percentage.

For many years, the people who promoted Victoria as a tourist destination compared the city to "a little bit of Old England." What did they mean by this? Granted, the scenery around Victoria is reminiscent of the rolling English countryside, complete with gnarled oak trees; we have many narrow winding lanes flanked by stone walls; we have stately old homes and castles, many with an Old World look; afternoon tea is a popular pastime; and even today you'll find a lot of people walking Victoria's streets in tweed caps and jackets. But what I think they were getting at is that our city is also well known for its haunted places—just like Old Blighty. You can't travel far in England before yet another haunted castle, pub, hotel, or church beckons you to visit. Ian Gibbs was born in England, so perhaps his interest in ghosts comes naturally. He certainly has captured this aspect of Victoria with his stories about Hatley Castle, the Bent Mast, Bard & Banker, the Empress Hotel, Bedford Regency Hotel, Christ Church Cathedral, and many other places that would make any British ghost hunter feel right at home. Not surprisingly, haunted tourism is a niche that is growing quickly in our city.

Katherine and John Maltwood moved to Victoria from England in the 1930s. I suspect they were drawn here by some of that "Englishness" I have described. But Katherine was also looking for something else—something not immediately apparent, except to someone like herself who was versed in the arcane lore of astrology, Druids, and ley lines. The Maltwoods had lived near Glastonbury, one of England's most supernatural places, famous as the final resting place of King Arthur, as the repository for the Holy Grail, and for the venerable thorn tree reputedly descended from a piece of the True Cross brought to England by Joseph of Arimathea. Mrs. Maltwood developed a theory that Glastonbury was at the centre of a giant zodiac radiating across the countryside, with Glastonbury Tor at the centre. All of this was part of the wider study being made at the time by other researchers about ley lines (lines of strong energy under the earth's surface) and places of earth magic. When the Maltwoods moved to Victoria they purchased a half-timbered house at Royal Oak reminiscent of a Cotswold cottage. Their selection of that site was not a random act: it just happens to be on one of the major ley lines running through Victoria. There Mrs. Maltwood planted a slip from the Glastonbury Thorn. She never really left this perfect place, and her ghost is a fixture at the restaurant that now occupies her former home.

Ley lines are associated with haunted activity, so it is not a coincidence that several of the stories in this volume are directly connected to the ley line Mrs. Maltwood found. A casual observer might think the sites are unrelated, but nothing could be further from the truth. Only a few blocks away from the Maltwood's former home is Elk Lake Drive, a setting for one of Ian's stories. If you follow the ley line in a southwesterly direction from there it will take you right past the Wilkinson Road Jail, another building featured in the book. The end of this ley line just happens to be at Fort Rodd Hill and Fisgard Lighthouse, whose ghostly stories Ian has also brilliantly documented.

Many years after Katherine Maltwood's death, Ian Gibbs had occasion to work in the diocese office of Christ Church Cathedral. He devotes an entire chapter to the precinct around the cathedral and his own experiences there. I'm sure it's not a coincidence that the office stands on the site of the former bishop's palace that previously was the home of the prominent Powell family. Dr. I. W. Powell's ancestors lived at Nanteos in Wales and were said to be keepers of the Holy Grail that had been smuggled out of Glastonbury by monks fleeing in advance of King Henry VIII's men. On the grounds of Christ Church Cathedral another Glastonbury Thorn has been planted. Next door to the cathedral is Pioneer Square, the old cemetery from 1855, where our Ghostly Walks guides have spent many hours telling stories about Adelaide Griffin and Robert Johnson; Griffin and Johnson have inspired two of my favourite tales, which I'm pleased Ian has included in his volume.

Is it happenstance there is so much ghostly activity in this one small area around the cathedral? Not at all! The answer is simple: the cathedral precinct is situated right on another ley line. As a result, the site was destined to be one of extremely strong energy. Ultimately it was the place where Ian had the first of his many encounters with spirits in Victoria.

Many threads are interwoven into Victoria's ghostly lore that Ian Gibbs so successfully incorporates in his book. It's no shock that he sensed the energy in the former bishop's chapel for reasons he explains in his story. It is equally unsurprising that Ian and other paranormal investigators have found many other strong links between Victoria's history and ancient connections to the paranormal realm. *Victoria's Most Haunted* reveals a fascinating glimpse of Victoria's spirit world and is an invaluable resource for those intrigued by this profoundly haunted city.

JOHN ADAMS
Ghostly Walks Tours, Victoria BC
February 2017

INTRODUCTION

VICTORIA IS HARDLY unique in that it is haunted. But there are several things that make the nature of Victoria's ghosts and hauntings unique. Before we get into that, though, we need to come to some type of understanding about what is a ghost. One of my careers is as a guide for Ghostly Walks in Victoria, and we ask this question at the start of some of our tours. The answers we get back will vary. Some will say spirit, soul, energy, Chi; others will even say nonsense. Regardless of the answers we receive, we know that human beings are run by electrical energy. It causes our hearts to beat, our brains to function, and our muscles to move. When we die, that energy goes somewhere—but *where* seems to be the great question. It's where our religions, belief systems, and contemplations diverge. For our purposes, we will consider the definition of ghost to be "energy left behind."

There are a number of reasons why Victoria has such a concentration of these energies. The first reason is geographic. Victoria was built on a type of bedrock called basalt, which is believed to hold onto energy longer than other types of bedrock. Water and salt are believed to both attract and trap energy. Being an island in the Pacific Ocean, our city has plenty of salt and plenty of water. Some also credit our high levels of ghostly energy to the existence of "ley lines" beneath the earth's surface. These lines are believed to be very powerful, especially when they intersect. Victoria has an uncanny number of intersecting ley lines all over the inner harbour/downtown area.

Another reason is history. Victoria is one of the oldest cities in Western Canada. Established through the fur trade, gold rushes, and the pursuit of British Columbia's abundant natural resources, it has a long colonial history. This often led to violent encounters, accidents, and murders. But under the colonial façade, Victoria also has incredibly rich First Nations culture. It is believed that the Lekwungen people have inhabited the Victoria area for over 8,000 years and their ghosts remain, even though traces of their original settlements have all but disappeared. The Lekwungen people did not bury their dead in the same way the Europeans did. They practised sky burial, which involved placing their dead in baskets or boxes and setting them high up in trees in a sacred grove. They also believed that their dead remained among the living, still involved in day-to-day life. This certainly left its imprint on the spiritual environment of this city. Victoria is also home to one of Canada's oldest Chinatowns—its colourful history has contributed significantly to the ghostly tales in this city. Combine all of these elements and you can see exactly why Victoria is one of Canada's and, perhaps, North America's most haunted cities.

WHILE YOU'LL GET to know some of the history behind Victoria's most haunted in these pages, you'll also experience these stories from the point of view of someone who was involved and in touch with the hauntings. I have what I like to refer to as a "spidey sense" when it comes to spirits or ghosts. I've always been able to pick up on things going on in a place spiritually. When

I was a kid I was told I was wrong. People accused me of making it up. I know this wasn't said to be cruel; those people were just not in tune with or aware of what was going on. But as I've aged, and since I've become more comfortable with my capacity to sense spirits, my abilities have increased. I've found they become more reliable the more I trust them. If I'm somewhere safe, those abilities are easily accessible and I can connect with the spirits around me. To be clear, however, I am not the guy to call if you are having a problem with something in your home. I may be able to sense it, and even figure out why it is acting the way it is, but my abilities are limited to helping the living get along with the dead. There are plenty of other people who can help you out; check out my website (www.ghoststoryguy.com) for a list. Even though I may not be able to solve your haunted problem, I love to hear ghost stories. If you have any to share, my contact information is included at the end of the book, or simply head to the website.

Throughout the book I have changed people's names. Anyone who asked for their name to be withheld has been given a pseudonym. Where the story involves private residences, the details have been kept deliberately vague to protect the privacy of the people involved. On that note, I'd like to add that the stories and experiences shared in this book are based on the author's collection of sources, including individuals whose experiences have led them to believe they have encountered phenomena of some kind or another. The stories are meant to entertain, and neither the publisher nor the author claim that these stories represent fact. Additionally, it is not the author's intention to influence anyone's beliefs; instead, the author's wish is that these stories will inspire, thrill, delight, and comfort.

JAMES BAY

DEADMAN'S POINT—
THE INN AT LAUREL POINT

BEFORE 1855, Deadman's Point—or what we now know as Laurel Point—was a sacred space for the Lekwungen, the First Nations people who first inhabited the area. They kept this place as a village of the dead and practised sky burial among the tall trees that covered the point. Sky burials involved laying out their dead in nature, allowing the elements to clean the flesh from the bones, and then carefully and respectfully gathering the bones and placing them in baskets and boxes, which they then put high up in the special and revered trees. Their village was across the harbour at Songhees Point, but this village of the dead was sacred. The First Nations believed that the dead never truly left; they stayed, and remained a part of village life. They were respected and kept in their own place so they could not interfere with the lives of the living; thus certain days were set aside to go to the place of sky burial and perform ceremonies to honour and respect the ancestors.

In 1885, Jacob Sehl, who had arrived in BC from Germany in 1858, decided the point was the perfect spot for a furniture factory. To build his factory, Jacob first needed to clear all of the trees. He hired a team, and as the trees came down, the men noticed the boxes and baskets of bones tumbling from the trees to the ground. They thought it was strange, but kept clearing.

The First Nations people took notice of this. In fact, they were so distraught when they saw what Jacob's men were doing that the chief of the Lekwungen sent a runner over to the point to find out what was going on. The runner quickly realized that these men were not doing this to bring upon themselves some kind of profound curse, but rather their actions were the result of genuine ignorance to the fact that they were destroying a burial ground. When the runner returned to the village and explained this to the chief, he immediately sent the women and children inland, far away from the point. He knew something bad was going to happen: you cannot disturb the bones and resting places of the ancestors without consequence.

After the trees were cut down, the boxes and baskets of bones that had fallen were thrown into a giant pile and unceremoniously set on fire. When the fire died down, anything that hadn't burned was shovelled into the ocean. No thought was given to the people they had disturbed or the souls they might have angered.

Mr. Sehl then built his furniture factory. It ran very well, until a rather unfortunate evening in January 1894. Jacob and his wife, Elizabeth, had retired for the evening when they saw wisps of smoke coming up through the heating vent. In no time at all, their house was engulfed in flames. Strangely, the factory, which was over a kilometre away, began burning at the same time.

Jacob and Elizabeth ran from their burning home. As they ran, Elizabeth noticed there seemed to be figures leaping and dancing in the flames. She called them "fire men," and claimed they were running their hands down the drapes and along the walls to make the fire burn faster. Jacob and Elizabeth barely escaped with their lives. Elizabeth never got over the horror of losing her house and almost losing her life at the hands of the dancing "fire men." In fact, she ended up losing her mind; within six months of the fire, forty-seven-year-old Elizabeth Sehl died.

Jacob, having lost everything, tried to restart his factory and bring on partners, but he was not able to do so. His business never recovered and the factory was never rebuilt.

The chunk of land, which people had started referring to as Sehl's Point after the fire, was then bought by Mr. William Pendray, who saw the site as a wonderful place to build a paint factory. He began to build in 1908. William was not concerned with ancient First Nations curses or vengeful ghosts, but he was concerned—understandably—about fire. He installed a fire suppression system that was quite revolutionary for the early 1900s. It mostly consisted of large iron pipes that hung down from the ceiling; if a fire began, the system could be turned on with a large crank that would flood the tubes with water, which would fall from the holes in the pipes and extinguish the fire below. It wasn't quite what we have come to expect of the fire safety systems we enjoy today, but it was certainly better than nothing.

William was very proud of his new paint factory. He was walking through it one day, making sure everything was just so and had been done correctly, when he heard one of the large iron pipes coming loose from the ceiling. It fell forty feet, landing directly on William's head. He was killed instantly. With Willliam Pendray gone, his eldest son, Ernest, was expected to take over the factory.

Ernest Pendray enjoyed many of the things young men enjoy, including a very fast horse and buggy. Ernest loved riding his horse and buggy around town, going just about as fast as he could go. One day as he approached the factory, his horse suddenly and inexplicably shied and stopped dead in its tracks. Ernest was thrown from the carriage and landed directly in front of his horse.

Just as suddenly as the horse had stopped, it started running again, the carriage still attached. It pulled forward and the heavy steel-rimmed carriage wheel ran directly over Ernest's neck. Unfortunately for Ernest, his head and his body were separated, and Ernest died in the driveway, right in front of the factory.

Unlike Jacob Sehl's unfortunate house, the Pendray family home is still standing. It is now known as the Gatsby Mansion and is part of the Huntingdon Manor Hotel, just 250 metres from where the paint factory used to stand. If you happen to work the front desk at the Gatsby Mansion, you will be briefed on the emergency protocol. This protocol has nothing to do with fire or earthquakes, but is instead all about room number five. Room five was the master suite when William Pendray was the owner and occupant of the house; it's now the honeymoon suite. If you would like to see a ghost, there's a good chance your wish will be granted if you stay in room five. Many times guests have woken up to see two heads hovering and circling around the bed, watching them. Back to the "emergency" or ghost protocol that you, as a staff member, have been briefed on: it has been put into place for guests who show up at the front desk in the middle of the night in their pyjamas (or less) demanding to be moved into a new room. As per the protocol, the guests are relocated immediately, with smiles and assurances, and given a free breakfast—because, of course, free breakfast solves everything.

If you are still interested in staying in the haunted room, it would be best not to try for an extra spooky night. Attempts to make a booking for Halloween will likely require you to be placed on a waiting list. It could be a few years before you have the chance to spend a haunted night with the two resident spirits—that is, those of William and Ernest.

The gracious and lovely Inn at Laurel Point now stands where Mr. Sehl and Mr. Pendray both had their ill-fated factories. The site was originally referred to as Deadman's Point, so I can see why the name would be changed: I'm not sure the inn would get many guests if they'd called it Inn at Deadman's Point. Please be assured: if you are staying there, you have nothing to fear. The vengeful spirits seem to have calmed down quite a bit. However, guests and staff have experienced dark shadows moving through the halls, wine glasses tipping over by themselves, and strange noises or sounds coming from empty rooms. While no one is overly anxious to discuss such things, you may notice them if you go there. While the ghosts have indeed settled down, they still remain.

My own experience over at the Inn at Laurel Point is quite typical. I knew nothing of its history or hauntings the first time I went there; I had been invited to a retirement event for a colleague. I remember being in a beautiful solarium at the back of the hotel. It struck me as very odd that the room seemed to be quite dim. Not only were the lights on, but also the sun was shining through the windows. I couldn't shake the feeling of darkness—not in an evil sense, just in an absence-of-light sense. Since my first experience in the hotel, I have been back a number of times for different events and occasions. It really is an excellent hotel, but I always notice a feeling of darkness that seems to permeate all of the public spaces.

I returned to the hotel recently with a friend who is also sensitive to spiritual things. Ensuring that we were both open and protected, we walked through the hotel and tried to absorb what was going on around us. We both sensed, almost at the same moment, a wistfulness or lostness that seemed to be the primary energy moving around us. Could this be the displaced spirits who'd had their eternal home disturbed and destroyed? As we explored the building, we almost seemed to be drawing some energy to us. Perhaps it could sense that we were there to experience something and was drawn to that. I am not sure, but after a while we felt it would better if we left. There is a sadness to the land and the building that is hard to explain. It is unfortunate that what was set aside as a sacred place of rest and honour was so badly defiled by newcomers who didn't know any better. Would this piece of land be quite so scarred if its original purpose had not been disrupted? In and around Victoria we come across this situation again and again. It may be why the spirits in Victoria are still so active and insist on being remembered and discovered even today.

THE BENT MAST

THE BENT MAST Restaurant & Lounge opened in 1995 in what was originally a private home. It seems like a strange spot for a house in modern-day James Bay, but the location makes more sense once you learn that it was one of the first houses to be constructed in the area. It was built in the 1870s and sits at the crossroads of Simcoe, Toronto, and Menzies Streets.

There have been multiple reports of strange goings-on at the Bent Mast. (Well, to be honest, around all of James Bay.) The first time I entered the building I sensed something—not just something but some *things*. The sensations are quite heavy throughout, but I didn't really have a sense of what or why until I went upstairs to use the washroom. It definitely feels like there's a woman up there. A cranky old woman—the kind who would brook no foolishness when she was alive and certainly resents anyone disturbing her space now. I did what I had to do and got out of there as quickly as I could. I could feel her frustrated eyes boring into me the whole time. Talk about disconcerting!

The servers have reported feeling like they've been pinched on the bum while the pub is empty. And no one likes going downstairs to change the beer kegs; one employee reported having the door close behind her when she was alone down there. The feeling in the basement is a male presence, and he's not very nice.

One of the most amazing incidents happened soon after one of the previous owners of the pub died. A group of men were out on the front patio talking about him. He was a character who could polarize a crowd; some in the group thought he was great, while others hadn't cared for him. One man spoke up with a negative opinion. When he finished his piece, he brought his beer mug up to his lips and just as he was about to take a sip, the mug suddenly shattered, covering the man with beer and broken glass. Apparently the former owner reciprocated that man's distaste.

Some people have reported being shoved or pushed as they were going down the stairs from the upper level washrooms. A friend of mine, Mike, had been enjoying a good time with friends in the pub. He wasn't drunk, but he'd had more than one beer. Mike said that as he came down the stairs, he was shoved hard. I asked him if he was sure that he hadn't just tripped and he said no way. He had felt two very distinct, smallish hands on his back, and then felt them give him a good hard shove. Thankfully, he was able to grab the banister and catch himself from falling, but it unnerved him.

Activity in the kitchen can sometimes be an issue as well: knives go missing, things tip over, and sometimes dishes slide off the counters by themselves and smash on the floor. All of this contributes to the overall spooky, but fun, atmosphere of the Bent Mast.

HELMCKEN HOUSE

ELMCKEN HOUSE WAS the home of Dr. John Sebastian Helmcken, Victoria's first and, for a long time, only doctor. The original house, which was added onto twice, was built in 1852 when Fort Victoria was still a tiny settlement of approximately three hundred people and the good doctor was twenty-six years old. Born in 1824 in the impoverished Whitechapel district of London, England, John Sebastian Helmcken worked his way through medical school by doing apprenticeships as a chemist and eventually gaining permission to become a medical pupil. He arrived in Victoria in 1850, an employee of the Hudson's Bay Company. He was well loved and well respected in the community; he fit right into the Fort's rough-and-ready lifestyle. By 1856, he had become the Speaker of the House in the British Columbia Legislature. In 1870, he was part of the three-man delegation sent to Ottawa to negotiate British Columbia's entry into Canada.

Obviously Dr. Helmcken was no ordinary country doctor. He married the daughter of the governor of BC in 1852, and cemented himself as a permanent part of the community to which he was determined to contribute. He and his wife, Cecilia, had seven children, of whom only four survived to adulthood. Sadly, the lovely Cecilia, to whom John was devoted, died of pneumonia at the age of thirty. They were only together for twelve years. People said that when Cecilia died the light went out of John's eyes.

Even though he lived to the age of ninety-six, he was never quite the same again, and he never remarried. In 1920, Dr. Helmcken died in the house he'd built for his wife and family. His daughter Dolly, who lived with him in his final years, also died in the house. It's believed that Dolly and Dr. Helmcken still inhabit the house, along with a few of the other children, who never had a chance to grow to adulthood, that Dr. Helmcken and Cecilia had.

Dr. Helmcken seems to take up residence in the master bedroom. While touring the house some visitors have seen a hand come around the door, then push it closed. Other people have smelled pipe smoke in the house, though no one has smoked inside it for many years.

On the Ghostly Walks tours I lead, we go into the backyard. As they walk past the back steps, some people are intimidated when they see a stern-faced lady standing on the stoop. This figure is assumed to be Cecilia, but it may also be Dolly. There are some who choose not to go in the backyard at all, as the spiritual energy is quite palpable. This could be because the three children who died in infancy were buried in the backyard, as would have been the custom of the day.

Andrea Bailey, founder of Unearthing Shadows Paranormal, graciously shared her own experiences of Helmcken House with me. When I asked her about the house, she told me:

> I've had a few stories there. Once I was sitting there [at the front of the house] after work, where I had met a friend. We were just talking, and I don't know why, but I kept looking into one window that had a curtain on it. There was no reflection and no one inside. Then I saw a head just above the curtains, and a shadow behind that walked from left to right and seemed to be a female. I asked

the security guard, who confirmed no one was inside. Unless someone walked right in front of us, which they didn't, there is no way the figure could have been an outside reflection either because it was coming from inside the home.

The other experience happened one evening when I was with two friends and we were walking back to my car. We stopped in the area, talking about the previous experiences we had at Helmcken House. I kept seeing a hefty, middle-aged woman, peering through a window in the room that's set up as the living room. Then I got really tired and felt like I was experiencing a panic attack. I felt like I wanted to get out of there. Then, before I said anything, the other person started saying he was feeling the same as me. We felt like someone was watching us, and they were angry we were there. I also kept getting flashes of a pissed-off woman in my mind. So we left. A security guard came by so we asked him if anyone was inside the house and he said no, there was no way anyone could be inside. He just did a walk through and locked it up a bit before we were there. I haven't been inside since I was a kid and I really don't even remember being inside, so weeks later when the museum opened the house up to the public, I walked in and was drawn to a picture in the living room. It was of the woman I physically saw and mentally saw. After this, others were contacting me about similar situations they were experiencing there.

When there are children on the Ghostly Walks tours, they will frequently notice something that a lot of the adults do not. The guide generally stands with their back to the house so the group has a clear view of the house. Often children will begin waving up at the window or playing hide and seek. When asked what they're doing, they respond with a chilling statement: "I'm waving at the girl in the window. She keeps waving at me."

Dolly was the spinster daughter who never left. She looked after her father until his death and eventually followed him to the grave, also dying in the house. Visitors to the house will often smell the strong smell of perfume, a scent known to have been favoured by Dolly. Dolly has even been known to give tours of the house, unbeknownst to the human visitors. One woman even went so far as to thank the security guard on duty and compliment the period-dressed woman who had shown her group around upstairs. The guard then had the uncomfortable job of letting the visitor know that there were no guides working that day. When the woman insisted, even describing the dress the woman had been wearing, the guard recognized it as a dress that hangs up in one of the sealed-off upstairs rooms.

A compelling story told by one of the actors in the Christmas re-enactment play, which is held annually in Helmcken House, is another reason to suspect Dolly is the strongest entity in the house. The group had hired all of their actors for the Christmas play, which was to depict the Helmcken family gathered at Christmas to celebrate the holiday together in a Victorian way. The actor who played Dolly had to be able to play the piano. Dolly was famous for her piano playing, and the actress was meant to play "Silent Night" at the end of the play. Unfortunately, the woman cast as Dolly fudged her piano ability in her audition, but she assured everyone involved she could play the song without any problem. In reality, the woman had no idea how to play the piano.

As opening night drew nearer, the rehearsal for the final scene revealed her secret to everyone. It was clear to all that there was no way this actor was going to be able to perform the song at the end of the play. Not only that, but there was no time to cast anyone else. The production team sent her to private and intensive music lessons to learn how to play that one song and only that one song. The actor tried, but she could not train her hands to play the song that quickly. Even at the final dress rehearsal, she was still butchering the song beyond belief. The cast decided they would just have to sing very, very loudly—sort of the opposite of "Silent Night"—and the actor would do the best she could. Everyone hoped the singing would cover up the terrible playing.

The night the play opened, everything went perfectly. The other actors were feeling a bit anxious as it came closer to the time when this poor woman would have to humiliate herself by playing a favourite and familiar Christmas song extremely poorly. The scene arrived, and the actor sat at the piano. She lifted her hands over the keys and began to play a beautiful, nuanced, and perfect version of "Silent Night." Thankfully the play featured excellent actors so their shock was well concealed, but no one could believe their ears. When the play was over and the audience had left, everyone gathered around the actor and asked her what had happened. She said she couldn't explain it, but it was as if someone else had taken over her hands and done the playing. It was the most amazing thing that had ever happened to her. The best part? This strange phenomenon recurred every night the play ran, but only during the actual performance. If the actor attempted to play the song at any other time, it sounded just as awful as it always did. But in front of an audience, there to relive the Helmcken family Christmas, it peeled off as beautifully and professionally as if done by a concert pianist. Apparently Dolly was not going to let her lovely family Christmas be remembered as anything other than perfect.

The house is open during the summer for tours and I would encourage you to go. Located beside the Royal British Columbia Museum in Thunderbird Park, it's a piece of local history as well as a wonderfully haunted building.

DOWNTOWN

THE EMPRESS

T HE GRANDEST OF Victoria's hotels is part of a national legacy of travel and tourism, a jewel of the Inner Harbour, and stuffed to the rafters with ghosts.

Seen within her walls are a construction worker in a hurry, a bellhop who never retired, a devout maid attending to her duties, a lost little old lady, and even Francis Mawson Rattenbury, the architect who designed the place and whose ghost still lingers, hoping to achieve the adulation he feels he so richly deserves.

The Empress was constructed between 1904 and 1908 as part of a chain of hotels built and maintained by the Canadian Pacific Railway to encourage tourism across Canada. Indeed, her sister hotels include the Banff Springs Hotel, the Château Frontenac in Old Quebec City, and the Royal York in Toronto. The Empress has never really known a time of completion as the first of two wings was added on to the hotel in 1909, only a year after it officially opened. The second wing was added in 1928, and the building seems to be under near-constant renovation.

The hotel has played host to many famous people, including movie stars and royalty. In 1919, Prince Edward danced in the Crystal Ballroom. King George and Queen Elizabeth dined there in 1939. For a city that at the time consisted of only thirty thousand people, this was a big deal. Celebrities of the day were also frequent visitors, and still are—but not as often under their own names. As well countless wealthy tourists looking to enjoy Victoria's views and amenities have frequented, and continue to visit, the hotel.

The Empress came close to being torn down in 1965 when the general consensus among Victorians was that the hotel had lost its lustre. Some felt it would have been better if a new and more functional hotel was put in its place. Given the architectural legacy left over from that era, the new hotel would probably have been vaguely prisonesque—concrete with tiny skinny windows—in the Neo-Brutalist fashion of many of the 1960s' buildings. Thankfully public outcry saved the grand hotel. Rather than being torn down, yet another renovation occurred, this one to the cost of 4 million dollars—the equivalent of more than 30 million today.

One of the first ghosts to not only haunt the hotel but also be created in it was that of chambermaid Lizzie McGrath. Lizzie was a woman in her middle to later years who had worked in some of the finest hotels in Ireland. When she saw the 1908 advertisement for this new hotel in Canada she felt like she needed to become a part of it. Little did she know how much of a permanent fixture she would become.

The advertisement calling for staff at the Empress Hotel said they were looking for the best of the best: the finest cooks, the finest maids, the finest hotel staff anywhere. Canadian Pacific needed to advertise for staff because back in 1908, there weren't enough experienced hotel staff in Victoria to meet CPR's demanding standards. The staff were recruited and eventually arrived from all over the Commonwealth to work in what was imagined to be the most magnificent hotel. Lizzie packed her bags and headed for a ship that took her over to Canada from Ireland.

After arriving in Montreal she boarded the train and headed out to British Columbia. Eventually arriving in Vancouver many days later, she boarded another ship, which took her to the Inner Harbour, where she would have had her first glance at the Empress. She was brought on as staff and given a room on the sixth floor of the hotel.

When the hotel first opened, it was quite common for the staff to live in the hotel. The sixth floor was assigned to the live-in staff. By all accounts, Lizzie was quite happy in her job: she enjoyed being in the grand hotel and working in the tea room, she loved living in Victoria, and she loved being able to look out her window on the sixth floor toward the Inner Harbour. Lizzie felt at peace. She knew leaving Ireland had been the right decision.

In 1909, the first of many renovations began. One of the first things that happened was that all of the drainpipes and fire escapes were removed so construction could begin on the exterior masonry and painting. If this had occurred in modern times, there would have been warning signs on the fire escape. There likely would have been bars across the door and everyone would have known there was nothing waiting to catch them on the other side. Unfortunately for our friend Lizzie, no such precautions were taken.

At the end of a long busy day, before she got ready for bed, Lizzie, a devout Roman Catholic, picked up her rosary and headed for the fire escape like she did every day. She pushed open the door, took one step forward, and fell six floors to her death.

Lizzie landed just to the right of where the main entrance to the hotel is now, in the back right-hand corner of the courtyard. She often appears where she fell, dressed in her black and white maid's uniform and clutching her rosary. Lizzie rushes from that corner and into the wall of what is now the entrance area. People have said that they have seen her lying there, quite content, quiet, and at peace. Lizzie is also sometimes seen going about her duties. Hotel guests will see a chambermaid walking along the hallway on the sixth floor, which has now been turned into guest rooms, and will call after her, perhaps to ask for more towels or have something done with their room. The front desk has gotten used to receiving phone calls from disgruntled tourists who say things like, "It's all very well to have chambermaids dressed in period costume, but if they're not going to do their job, what is the point?" The front desk staff then tries to smooth over the situation and sends up a real-life room attendant, but they don't go into a lot of detail about who the mysterious and possibly deaf chambermaid might be. By all accounts Lizzie is at peace; she smiles at people as she passes them, and nods her head. It is nice to think that a chambermaid from 1909 who could have easily been forgotten is still remembered and is still a part of her beloved hotel.

DURING A RENOVATION in 2016, two painters, one of whom was named Troy Reid, were working on the second floor. They were in separate rooms, but they each had the door to their room open. They both heard a noise at the same time and looked out their doors to the hall, where they saw an Indigenous construction worker running quickly down the hallway. They stopped what they were doing and stepped into the hallway. The pair was concerned because there had to be a good reason for any construction worker to run down a hall. There could be a fire or a flood or a gas leak; when someone runs on a renovation site, you really do want to know why. They tried to follow the man, but the hall was a dead end. There was nowhere the man could have gone. They walked to the end of the hall themselves to make sure all of the doors were locked and no one else was there. They looked at each other and asked, "Did you see that?" Troy and his partner both agreed they had. Was it a construction worker from a long-ago job who never got to complete his work? Did he attempt to run from what eventually killed him? Troy later discovered that it was indeed the spirit of a First Nations worker. One had been killed in a renovation back in the 1970s on the same floor they had been working on when he fell out a window he had been repairing.

IN THE 1950S, the Empress Hotel was mostly empty during the winter. There were no direct flights to Victoria, and there were not yet daily ferries between Victoria and mainland BC in the winter, making Victoria a bit of a "ghost" town during the cold months. There were certainly ways to travel here but it wasn't as easy nor was the transportation as frequent as it is now. To help fill the vacancies, the ingenious managers of the hotel decided to drop the rates and advertise a winter stay at the Empress to people living in other parts of Canada. As Victoria gets very little snow, this was an attractive prospect for anyone seeking to escape snowbound homes. Margaret, a woman from Calgary, particularly enjoyed coming to Victoria for the winter and made a habit of doing so every year. She would lock up her house just after Christmas, travel to Victoria, and then remain at the hotel until April or May. She became such a well-known visitor that the staff knew her by name. Margaret was a very ritualistic person. She stayed in the same room each year. By this point in the hotel's history, the sixth floor had been converted from staff rooms into guest rooms and Margaret's room was on the sixth floor on the far left-hand side of the hotel, in the tower that had been added in 1929.

She also steadfastly maintained the same schedule each day. Margaret could always be relied upon to show up for afternoon tea at four o'clock. One afternoon, Margaret did not come down for tea. When evening fell and she still hadn't turned up, a manager went to check on her, wondering if perhaps she was ill or if she had gone out (which was highly unlikely). He knocked on the door three times without any response, so he used a passkey to enter the room. There he found Margaret in bed; she had obviously laid down for a nap before tea time and was never going to wake up.

Hotels do not close a room simply because someone has died in it. They will clean the room, flip over the mattress, and rent it out as soon as it's ready. Most of the time, this is not an issue; however, sometimes hotels end up with an interesting phenomenon known as "the unrentable room." It's what the hotel industry calls the overflow room. The only way this room is rented out is if nothing else is available in the hotel. Margaret's former room became the Empress's unrentable room. Anytime that room was rented out, it usually ended up being more of a headache for the front desk than it was worth.

One couple who ended up in this particular room was a middle-aged husband and wife from Manitoba. They had come to Victoria for an anniversary celebration. They were enjoying their visit immensely, but the wife, tired from her wanderings around the city, decided to take a little break before going down for dinner. She climbed into the bed and turned on the television. Suddenly the channel changed. Grabbing the remote, she changed it back to what she had been watching; within a few minutes, the channel changed back again. Frustrated, she gave up and read her book instead. After dinner, the couple retired for the evening. They tucked themselves into bed and turned off the lights. Just as they were starting to drift off to sleep, they heard footsteps very close to the bed. Then the bathroom light flipped on, but no one was there. The husband and wife looked at each other. It was one of those are-you-seeing-what-I'm-seeing moments of disbelief, but it was clear the bathroom light was on. Then they heard water running in the sink, and then the toilet being flushed. The bathroom light clicked off, and the sound of shuffling feet came towards the bed. To their horror, the couple felt the covers pull back and something cold climb into the bed with them. At this point, they got up and requested another room.

Eventually, as the style and tastes changed for guests, the hotel realized the two large storage areas in the towers above the sixth floor had the finest views of the Inner Harbour. It seemed ridiculous to store old furniture and things that the hotel no longer required in a space that could fetch a premium. By this point, the entire hotel staff knew about the overflow room. They also knew about the ghost that had been seen in the 1960s in the storage area, where one of the former employees, having lost his job, had hanged himself from a rafter on the eighth level. But once the hotel management realized they could convert the storage spaces into luxury accommodations, to be christened the Gold Suites, they quickly started to plan.

The main problem with the conversion was that the elevator in the hotel only went up to the sixth floor. No hotel would ask guests who are paying for the most expensive rooms to carry their luggage up two flights of stairs, so the Empress decided to add an exclusive elevator to take guests from the sixth to the seventh and eighth floors. This led to the conundrum of where to put the elevator, but the ingenious managers soon found a solution. Why not kill two birds with one stone, so to speak, and turn the unrentable room into a private elevator for the Gold Suite guests? The room was taken apart; the wall was removed and the elevator was installed. The management congratulated themselves on not only getting rid of the unrentable room but also creating more revenue for the hotel with the Gold Suites.

But if the managers thought they were getting off that easy, they were mistaken.

Not long after the elevator was installed, more guests on the sixth floor began experiencing a strange phenomenon. Imagine: you are getting ready to go to sleep, then you hear a light, timid knocking at the door—not a commanding I'm-here-from-the-front-desk sort of sound, just a tapping that is barely audible. When you open the door, you find a nice old lady standing in the hallway—which feels unnaturally cold—in her slippers and her robe looking confused. When you ask this lady how you can help her, she says she is terribly sorry to bother you, but she is unable to find her room. She tells you her room number and then, as most people would, you offer to help her find her room. She follows you down the hallway making small comments and apologies. You can hear her shuffling behind you, and when you get to the place where her room should be, you realize there is no room there: it's merely a boutique elevator. You turn to speak to her to suggest that perhaps she has forgotten her room number or has it wrong, but to your surprise, she is no longer there. You know without a doubt that you heard her shuffling behind you, but she has vanished. Unfortunately for the hotel management, rather than getting rid of Margaret, they have instead set her wandering, perpetually seeking a room to which she can never return.

ANOTHER GHOSTLY ENCOUNTER was shared by a young couple who were on their honeymoon in the 1980s. They checked in on

Christmas Eve, and as anyone in the hotel industry can tell you, hotels are usually understaffed at Christmas. There was no one to take their bags, but they didn't mind—they simply started hauling their luggage to their room. As they approached the elevator, a porter came seemingly out of nowhere. He was dressed in a red jacket and blue pants that had gold braiding down the side; his nametag identified him as Bill. Bill was an older man, and looked as if he may have enjoyed a drink or two, but he happily took their bags to their room. The couple walked into the room ahead of him. When they turned around to tip him, he was gone, but their bags were at the door of their hotel room. The couple was puzzled and wondered why he hadn't waited for a tip. Aware that the hotel was short-staffed they finally assumed he'd been called to help out elsewhere. They put the money for his tip aside, intending to take it down to the front desk to ensure Bill received it. The next day was Christmas, and they forgot to leave it at the desk in the midst of the holiday and their time together.

Again, on Boxing Day, the hotel was quite empty of staff and the couple didn't think of Bill's tip. On December 27, as they were packing to leave, they came across the envelope with Bill's tip in it. They went to the front desk and asked if they could leave the envelope for the porter named Bill who had assisted them on Christmas Eve. The front desk clerk apologized, but informed the couple they didn't believe anyone named Bill worked at the hotel. The young couple insisted that Bill had kindly helped them on Christmas Eve when there weren't any other porters around and they wanted to ensure that he got their tip. The front desk clerk, hoping to help out in any way, called the captain of the porters to come and assist the guests. The young couple told the man what they were trying to accomplish and why. The captain of the porters, dressed in an entirely different uniform—olive green, no hat—looked a little confused and asked, "What did he look like?" The couple described Bill, saying he was older and had a rather red nose, but he was helpful and very pleasant when he took their bags to their room. The captain looked uncomfortable and then explained that there had been a porter named Bill, but unfortunately he had passed away many years ago when the captain himself was a junior porter. Bill most certainly enjoyed a drink or two on a regular basis and, unfortunately, his health was poor. Bill had passed away one day while working at the hotel. The young couple thanked the captain. They left the tip with him, but took away an amazing story of a paranormal encounter.

If your bags are taken to your room as you check into the Empress, maybe look twice at who is carrying them. Is he wearing the customary modern uniform of the porters, or does his outfit look like an old-fashioned uniform that may have been seen a number of years ago?

FRANCIS MAWSON RATTENBURY was a well-known architect responsible for many of Victoria's most iconic buildings and homes, including the parliament buildings and the Steamship Terminal, directly across from the parliament buildings.

When Rattenbury was a young architect, he won the competition to design the parliament buildings. With such a large commission under his belt, he was soon in high demand to design many other buildings in Victoria, including the Empress. Many adjectives can be used to describe Rattenbury, but confident is probably the kindest.

Rattenbury, as it turned out, was not a very nice man. He was the most celebrated architect in Victoria during his era, the 1890s to 1920s, partly because his wife Florence, or Florrie, as she was called, was beloved by anyone who met her. Where Francis could be cold and dismissive, Florrie was attentive and kind, always going out of her way for someone in need or someone who needed cheering up. Francis, on the other hand, could be counted on to only do what was right for him and him alone. When Francis was in his mid-fifties, he met a woman named Alma. At twenty-six years old, Alma was fun and flashy; she played the piano with enthusiasm and skill, and was a good-time girl of the highest order. Francis told Florrie that he needed a divorce because he had fallen in love with Alma. Florrie refused to give him a divorce on the grounds that she would be humiliated and ruined in the eyes of everyone in the community, but he didn't care. Francis flaunted his affair with Alma. He moved into a hotel room with her and took her to all of his social events, leaving his wife at home, alone and isolated. As an added act of spite, and to encourage his wife to give him the divorce he so sorely wanted, he had the power and heat turned off at the home they had shared, leaving his wife and two children in the dark and the cold. Francis's treatment of Florrie was so horrendous that his friends and former clients shunned him. They turned the other way when they saw him coming, and all of his invitations to Victoria society events dried up.

In 1925, Florrie finally agreed to grant him a divorce, if for no other reason than to protect her children and be rid of him and his cruelty. Francis thought his life would return to normal but not only had his social life become non-existent, his architectural business had as well. Finally realizing he had effectively destroyed his life in Victoria, he moved back to England with Alma in 1929. That same year, long-suffering Florrie died.

In England, Alma found herself in a situation she had not bargained for. Rather than enjoying the pinnacle of society, she found her life revolved around an increasingly elderly gentleman. Alma was bored and she tired of living with him. Francis and Alma had hired an eighteen-year-old chauffer named George, who, by popular reporting, was a few sandwiches short of a picnic. In the early hours of March 23, 1935, Francis Rattenbury was discovered in a gruesome state. He had been so severely beaten about the head with what appeared to be a carpenter's mallet that part of his skull had detached from the back of his head. He died a few days later. Alma confessed immediately, but George told one of the housemaids that he had in fact been the one to deliver the blows. Both Alma and George were taken to prison and subsequently tried. Alma was acquitted, but young George was sentenced to death. On the day she was acquitted, Alma went to a riverbank and stabbed herself six times in the chest and threw herself in the water. A capital punishment sentence did not, of course, mean that George was immediately put to death; there were appeals and appeals of the appeals to get through first. Ironically, only seven years into this process, George was released to join the army and fight in the Second World War. Upon his return, he married, had a child, and lived a pretty quiet life.

In the meantime, it appears that the spirit of Francis Rattenbury has come back to the place of his greatest glory: the Empress. Rattenbury can often be seen loitering around the stairs where his picture hangs, as if waiting for passing guests to notice him and heap praise on him for what a wonderful job he has done on the hotel. Perhaps he's waiting for someone to recognize him and invite him to an event. He also appears in the basement around the washrooms. His appearance is more common when there is regular traffic. You might suppose he is interested in speaking to people, but as soon as you look at him and try to speak, he disappears or walks into a wall where once there was a door.

The sheer number of ghosts who have remained at the Empress says a great deal about its beauty, style, and ability to build loyalty. If you are privileged enough to stay within its walls, keep your eyes and ears open. You may have a chance to interact with more than just the employees still on the payroll or your fellow guests.

THE BEDFORD REGENCY HOTEL—THE CHURCHILL AND GARRICK'S HEAD PUB

THE BUILDING THAT is now the Bedford Regency Hotel has certainly seen some changes since it was built to house the local newspaper, the *British Colonist*, in 1873. When the newspaper left the property in 1898, it was bought by Mr. Thomas Hibben and his partner, Mr. Bone. The duo purchased the two-storey building with plans to turn it into a book and stationery shop. In 1911, Mr. Hibben hired architect Thomas Hooper, who incidentally designed many other haunted buildings in the downtown core, to add three storeys to create an office building. This office building was a great idea at the time, and it aimed to attract the lawyers and law firms that were flocking to be close to the Supreme Court of British Columbia courthouse in Bastion Square, which had been built in 1889. The board of trade had also built a new office in Bastion Square that was intended for all of British Columbia. Bastion Square was the place to be and the newly improved Hibben-Bone Block was in a perfect location to capitalize on that fact.

Unfortunately for the newly expanded building, dark times lay ahead. The First World War and prohibition effectively sank the city of Victoria into a depression between 1914 and 1921. First World War restrictions were put on most of the land, so coal and lumber barons packed up and went to Vancouver. During prohibition, the hotels around Bastion Square could not afford to stay open without saloons, so many of them closed. A lot of office buildings ended up being used to store furniture or accept shipments that were coming in from the docks. In an effort to continue to make a profit, the building went through a succession of lives as different hotels. The Bedford Regency was once known as the Bastion Inn, the Alhambra Hotel, and, at its most infamous, the Churchill Hotel. The Churchill Hotel was open from the 1940s to the 1970s. Its roughest and most notorious time occurred in the 1960s when the new courthouse opened on Blanshard Street in 1961. At that time, many Victorians viewed the rundown and dilapidated Bastion Square area as ready to meet the wrecking ball.

The Churchill was a disreputable destination in the 1960s. It was well known for its beer parlour in the basement, its biker clientele, the friendly professional ladies, and, of course, the run-of-the-mill thugs and drunkards. The bar was so infamous that legend says there was a particular biker who became upset enough that he drove down the steps into the bar from Government Street on his motorbike.

Two of the most famous characters from the Churchill were featured on a segment of a television show called *Creepy Canada*. Their names were Brady and Charlotte, or Lady Churchill as she was known. Brady worked at a local radio station in the 1960s and by all accounts had a face for radio. He was a big man and what people always remembered about him was the ever-lit cigar clamped firmly in his mouth and the cloud of cigar smoke that surrounded him. Charlotte worked in the hotel. That is, she rented room number forty-nine in the hotel and entertained gentleman clients there.

Charlotte was a creature of habit. Every afternoon around four o'clock, she would head down to the beer parlour and have half a pint of whatever was on tap. It was also a good opportunity for Charlotte to meet potential or current customers. Everyone knew when Charlotte was there as she too was known by a signature scent: a strong, cheap floral perfume, in which she seemed to douse herself every morning.

As fate would have it, Charlotte and Brady met down in the bar one afternoon and hit it off. Soon they were spending quite a bit of time together and Brady made the progression from customer to favourite customer, then to heavily discounted customer, and suddenly—to everyone's amazement—fiancé. Brady and Charlotte spent a lot of time talking about the new life they would have in Vancouver, usually over breakfast on the weekends. However, not everyone in the beer parlour was happy about their relationship. There was one patron who was, in fact, very upset. It is assumed he was a client or former client of Charlotte's who was upset that she was no longer offering her charms. He was so angry that one afternoon when Brady came to meet Charlotte for her four o'clock drink, the former customer confronted Brady. They exchanged some words and as Brady rallied to the defense of his fiancée, the furious man got even angrier. He told the courts later that he'd only meant to scare Brady, but he'd been drinking. He smashed a beer bottle on the edge of the bar and thrust it at Brady's face. Instead of merely threatening Brady, the man slashed the carotid artery in Brady's neck. Brady turned to climb the steps up to Government Street, but he didn't get very far. One person was quoted as saying: "Everyone knew Brady was dead when the cigar he always had lit rolled down the stairs and extinguished itself in a pool of his blood."

When Charlotte came down, she quickly discovered her fiancé, and perhaps the one hope of changing her life, was gone. Within a few weeks, Charlotte herself was gone. Unbeknownst to most of the people who knew her, Charlotte was addicted to heroin. One night when she was alone in her room, she overdosed and was later discovered dead.

The years rolled by and the Churchill finally closed in the late 1970s. It was purchased, renovated, and reopened as the Bedford Regency. Ironically, room forty-nine, Charlotte's room, was expanded and turned into the bridal suite. People staying there have experienced a shimmering light in front of the door before they put their key card in. There have been many reports of singing coming from the room, even when it's empty. Other times the poor occupant has been in the bathroom and heard singing in the main part of the room. What is always present when Charlotte is around is the unmistakable scent of a strong, cheap floral perfume.

One night, two of the Ghostly Walks guides were doing a tour together. A mother and daughter approached the guide who was standing at the back of the group while the other guide told the ghost story about the Bedford Regency. The little girl pointed to the fourth floor and asked if the hotel had a ghost in it. The guide explained that the other guide was in the midst of telling the story of that very hotel and that very floor. The girl explained that she and her mother were staying in room forty-seven, and she kept hearing the sound of a woman singing from the room across the hall, room forty-nine, but when she asked the front desk about it, she was told there was no one staying in that room. At least they had confirmation that the girl was right, even if they didn't get a good night's sleep.

When the hotel was renovated, the new owners, rather wisely, decided not to reopen the basement as a beer parlour. Instead, they stripped out the bar components and made it into a staff room. One morning in the late 1980s, a man approached the front desk and said that he used to be a bartender in the beer parlour. He asked if there was any chance he could see what the old place looked like now. One of the room attendants overheard and invited him down to have coffee with her so he could see his old place of employment. The gentleman accompanied the woman down to the old bar and was introduced to the other staff sitting at the table. They hadn't been down there very long when everyone noticed the distinctive odour of cigar smoke. One of the room attendants looked over to the old stairs that led up to Government Street. The doors at the top were not only locked, but chained up. The attendant saw a man, as solid as any normal man, coming down the stairs. He was a large figure, and she said she could see cigar smoke around him, or so she thought. He appeared so real that she actually forgot the doors were unusable and stood up. She said, "Excuse me, but we're no longer open down here as a bar."

The man coming down the stairs simply vanished, but the smell of cigar smoke remained. The former bartender went pale and quietly said, "I know who that was." It was, of course, the unfortunate Brady, who must have come back to check out the old bar as well, or perhaps his spirit was drawn there by the former bartender whom he had known and seen every day.

One of the current staff members, Andrew, had been the night custodian at the Bedford Regency for about a year when I asked if he had any stories for me. I was not disappointed. Andrew's duties include cleaning the hotel and the attached Garrick's Head Pub. Built in 1867, the Garrick's Head is one of the oldest English pubs in Canada. Andrew explained he has experienced all kinds of phenomena in and around the hotel and pub. There is a back staircase to the hotel where Andrew has heard footsteps coming and going when no one is around. One night Andrew was alone in the pub after it had closed for the night. He was cleaning the men's bathroom in the basement of the pub. While he was in a stall, the tap on the right-hand sink suddenly turned on full blast. Andrew turned around as soon as he heard the tap, but no one else was in the bathroom. He turned off the tap and left the bathroom, deciding he would finish cleaning later on.

Andrew said that the maintenance man has also experienced strange phenomena. He complains that items and equipment have been moved around in his workshop, a place to which he is the only keyholder. The maintenance man also told Andrew that he has witnessed fully formed apparitions floating into walls. This actually makes some sense as the hotel has been remodeled so many times there are walls where doors used to be and vice versa. You will often see spirits behaving in the same way they would have during their own lifetimes. Sometimes when Andrew is mopping up in the Garrick's Head late at night, he will see two figures in the booth by the fireplace. They're usually talking and he can hear their voices, but he cannot quite make out what they're saying. Andrew has also experienced cold spots heading downstairs; he has smelled cigar smoke in the old beer parlour, and heard footsteps and glasses clinking.

The original owner of the Garrick's Head, Michael Powers, was murdered in 1899. He was coming home to the pub, which he lived above, around three AM when he was hit from behind with a five-pound sack of sand. Powers went down hard and was then beaten mercilessly. He was taken to the Royal Jubilee Hospital and died four days later from a ruptured liver; he never named his attackers. Police records show that one of the people involved in the attack may have been a woman dressed as a man. Michael was a hard-living, hard-drinking kind of guy, and not the sort of man to keep his opinions to himself. Records show that he clashed with local prostitutes about meeting customers in his pub, and he very publicly disparaged a local woman who was a well-known beauty and whose husband was often out of town. This woman was not a prostitute, but she did work in a local hotel. Michael had brought up her lack of fidelity more than once. It's doubtful we will ever know who decided to take Michael's life, but there was no lack of suspects.

Guests have also reported strange happenings. The glass of the old-school fire extinguisher cabinet once spontaneously shattered when no one had been near it; the scene was caught on a surveillance camera. Guests have also reported hearing running in the hall, so loudly and so often that they open their doors to see what the commotion is but nothing is there. People have reported hearing voices singing or laughing, and doors opening and closing on their own—all of the standard things you expect to experience in a haunted location.

As for Andrew, he accepts all of this for what it is, but sometimes he admits he gets a bit freaked out (once he heard the voice of a child ask him his name and if he wanted to play). Luckily Andrew is interested in ghostly things, so he has picked a great place to work.

When I spent time in the hotel, it was in the newly renovated pub on the main floor called the Churchill. It's a great place with great food and fast service. I felt nothing really strange there, but when I went out into the hotel proper to use the bathroom, I definitely felt some unrest. The main floor washrooms aren't that bad; if you're not sensitive to this sort of thing, you probably wouldn't even notice the unrest. When I was in the Garrick's Head, however, it was a different story. I could feel at least three presences around me, and the basement washrooms had me looking over my shoulder. I would have loved to go into the old beer parlour in the basement, but that is no longer a public space. I totally believe Andrew when he tells me there is a cigar-smoking presence down there. After the other things I've sensed in the hotel, how could there not be?

THE BARD & BANKER

THIS BUILDING IS a staple of Ghostly Walks tours, and is one of the best stories to tell. The building that is now the Bard & Banker pub was originally built as the Canadian Imperial Bank of Commerce in 1855 and was designed by the same architect, Warren H. Williams, as the Craigdarroch Castle. When this story took place, banks employed young men as tellers; part of their job was to live above the bank so they could be used as security if need be. The men understood they were expected to protect the bank and ensure the money remained where it was supposed to: in the vault.

There was a young man who worked for the bank who was very superstitious. He was so superstitious that he avoided walking past the bank's neighbour, a funeral parlour. This young man, named Robert, would go out most nights to the pubs down on Wharf Street. Even though the quickest way home was to walk up Government Street and past the funeral parlour, he wouldn't do it. He would take the long way round so he could approach the bank from another direction and avoid the funeral parlour altogether.

One night, Robert couldn't face the long way around as the town was being lashed by a major storm. As he made his way up Government Street, he noticed something that filled him with dismay. The door to the funeral parlour was open and there were lights moving around in the corner closest to the bank. Robert immediately assumed that criminals—who were actually funeral home workers—were taking advantage of the storm to break into the vault through the unprotected wall of the funeral parlour. He knew it was up to him to stop it.

Robert inched his way in, planning to take the robbers by surprise. It was pitch black inside. He felt his way slowly and surely toward the source of the light. Suddenly, he tripped over something on the floor and fell forward. He landed on something quite spongy. As he fell, he let out a cry and the men, gathered in the corner, rushed over with their lanterns to see what was happening. Their lamps illuminated a ghastly scene: Robert was face to face with a corpse.

During the storm, the steamship S.S. *Clallum* had foundered and gone down, taking fifty-five people with her, including many women and children. The ship had been running for less than a year and was on the Tacoma–Seattle–Port Townsend–Victoria route. When she was launched, the bottle of christening champagne missed the bow, and when her flag was unfurled for the first time, it was upside down, which is the universal sign for distress. Both incidents were seen as bad signs. The S.S. *Clallum* made her maiden voyage in July of 1903 and she sank in a storm on January 8, 1904. The storm had been dumping corpses on to the local beach all day. The funeral parlour had run out of room, so they had resorted to setting people out on the floor for identification the next day. Poor Robert was terrified of anything to do with death, and there he was lying within kissing distance of a drowned man. The dead man's eyes and mouth were open, as if gasping for one last breath, and his lips were a horrible shade of blue. Robert picked himself up and ran out of the funeral parlour and into the bank. But if he thought his experience was over, he was wrong.

Unfortunately for Robert, every time he closed his eyes, he saw the faces of the drowned shipwreck victims. This soon led to a lifelong issue with insomnia. Very soon he wanted out of Victoria; there were just too many reminders of the worst night of his life. When Robert approached his boss about transferring to a different branch, there was only one place available. The bank had opened up a new branch to accommodate a recent gold rush. It was located in Dawson City in the Yukon. There were not many people, other than those searching for gold, who were excited to go to the far north. Robert went, but his insomnia followed. He started to write poetry to give him something to do during the night. The verse (as he called it) became longer. Soon he was writing some significant pieces, including "The Cremation of Sam McGee" and "The Shooting of Dan McGrew." Robert Service became one of Canada's most celebrated poets.

Sometimes ghosts don't haunt where they died. Sometimes they return to significant places in their lives where they feel an emotional tie, or where they had a life-changing experience. One of these ghosts haunts the Bard & Banker. This presence was first noted in 1958 by a woman named Lily. Lily lived across the street from the building and taught weaving in her room, which was in an old hotel on Government Street. She was distressed by the fact that a man on the upper floor of the bank was standing at the window, staring straight into her room. This happened night after night. Finally Lily was so unnerved that she called the police. They spoke with the bank staff, who apologized but explained that the upper rooms were no longer in use. The police did their job and asked to see the room that was causing so much distress. Sure enough, upon investigation it was clear to the officers that no one had been in any of the upstairs rooms for quite some time. The dust had not been disturbed; no human being had been in there for ages, at least not a live one.

It didn't take long for someone to connect the dots. In the 1950s, a keen reporter from *Harper's Bazaar* had gone to the south of France, where Robert Service had been living and eventually died. He wanted to interview Robert specifically about his wild and exciting life in the Yukon. Unfortunately, Robert, then in his eighties, was only interested in talking about his time in Victoria and his face-to-face encounter with a recently drowned corpse. The poor reporter wasn't able to pry much more out of Robert, so the story became part of the feature. Coincidentally, one of Lily's students remembered reading the article and was able to explain to Lily who she was probably seeing.

I'm not sure how much comfort the information brought Lily, who now knew she was being watched by a ghost, but it certainly helped when it came time to choose a name for the pub, which opened in 2007. Robert Service was both a bard and a banker; the pub is named after him. If you visit the pub, there is a real possibility that you might feel Robert on the stairs; he is sometimes seen descending the staircase through the middle of the pub, although not as often anymore. His bank is a bit more crowded than he'd like. But there are still reports of people seeing him in the upstairs window on the far left. If you really want to see a ghost, though, this may be one way to do it: go into the pub, find a seat, and ask your server for a bottle of Robert Service Ale. His picture is on the bottle.

ROGERS' CHOCOLATES

IN 1885, THIRTY-ONE-YEAR-OLD Charles Rogers moved to Victoria to become a green grocer. He married a local girl named Leah, who was twenty-one at the time. Together they attempted to run their business. They quickly realized that while they had customers, they couldn't get truly fresh fruit and vegetables. For the most part, the vegetables weren't a problem; carrots, potatoes, and turnips have an exceptionally long shelf life. But the soft fruit, things like strawberries, raspberries, peaches, and plums did not fare as well on the long journey to Vancouver Island. Charles and Leah began to take the almost-spoiled fruit, dip it in sugar, coat it in dark chocolate, and then put it out for sale. To say they had a hit on their hands was an understatement. Every morning they opened their store with fully stocked shelves, and within forty-five to sixty minutes they would be sold out. Once Charles invented the Victoria Cream, there was no looking back. Rogers' Chocolates, with Charles running the business side and Leah in charge of the storefront, was a genuine success. They worked together to make the chocolates and created one of Canada's first world-famous brands. Queen Victoria herself was quite the fan and many boxes of chocolates were shipped to England and around the globe.

In 1903, a new building was built to house the business; the architect was our friendly neighbourhood haunted building creator, Thomas Hooper. And Rogers' Chocolates still uses that same store today, more than a century later. Naturally the building is profoundly haunted, and not just by Charles and Leah. Even though Charles and Leah were successful business people, excellent city leaders, and church-going folks, they were not the most attentive parents.

Freddie Rogers was born in 1890 to his very happy parents. Freddie was their only child, but sadly, they were so consumed by their business that they had very little time for Freddie. It wasn't that Freddie was neglected—they hired various nurses and governesses for him—but none of them stayed long. In today's terms we would understand that Freddie was simply acting out to gain attention from his absent parents. Back then, Freddie would have simply been known as a rotten child. One of Freddie's favourite things to do was blow things up. This sounds a bit extreme, and nearly impossible for a small child, but in the late 1800s, it was quite common for parents to send their children to the local hardware store to pick up all kind of things required around the farm or homestead, including dynamite for removing stumps or rocks from the property. Freddie enjoyed purchasing the explosive in sticks and then cutting them up into delightful "fun size" pieces. He would climb on the streetcar that ran along Government Street, pay his nickel, and remain standing near the front of the train. Once people had registered that he wasn't moving to a seat, he would pull out his mini dynamite stick and light the fuse. Standing there, watching people grow increasingly concerned, Freddie would wait until the very last second to fling it out the door of the moving streetcar, where it would explode mid-flight and cause mayhem both inside and outside the car. In the ensuing hysteria, Freddie would slip from the car and bolt up a side street, undoubtedly to cackle at the mess he had created. Freddie got so famous for doing this that the city actually passed a law prohibiting anyone named Frederick Rogers from using public transportation. Charles and Leah attempted to address this issue with their son, but the business always drew them back. Freddie was inevitably left to his own devices, running amok and causing panic and destruction wherever he happened to end up.

Eventually, when Freddie was fourteen years old, his luck ran out. During one of his many exploding adventures in the woods surrounding the town, he mistimed an experiment and was far too close to an explosion. He ended up permanently damaging his right hand so that it resembled more of a crab claw; he also lost the hearing in his right ear and the vision in his right eye. There is some speculation that he also experienced some brain damage because Freddie never got over these injuries. In January of 1905, Freddie, at the age of fifteen, checked in to the New England Hotel. Using a borrowed revolver, he took his own life. Charles and Leah were devastated and began to withdraw from the life they'd built in the community. They focused all of their attention on the business. They were so attached to their business that they stopped going home to their house in James Bay at the end of the workday. Instead, they brought two wicker chairs from home to the shop and hung them on the back wall of the candy kitchen. When night fell and their work was done for the day, the Rogers would unhook the chairs from the wall and place them on either side of the cooling candy stove. There they would rock quietly and grab a few hours of sleep before getting up and beginning the day's production. Their only real home was the candy kitchen and the upstairs office of the building on Government Street. Lost in their grief, they rarely left the store. As the years went by, the business did well, but Charles and Leah were never the same.

Things went on this way for the next twenty-two years. Charles died in 1927, and the business was too much for Leah to run on her own, so she sold the shop. She also had an estate of over 300,000 dollars, which Charles had left her, equivalent to more than 1.3 million dollars today. She moved to a small house in James Bay, and gave all of her money to the church and various charities around town. When Leah passed away in 1958 at the age of eighty-eight, she was living in poverty in a house with no electricity. In fact, there wasn't even money for a grave marker for her grave in the Ross Bay Cemetery. When the hauntings at the shop increased almost immediately after her death, Rogers' Chocolates purchased a stone for Leah in hopes that she would leave them alone. It didn't work, but it was still a kind thing for the company to do.

The hauntings had begun soon after Charles died. He was the candy maker of the couple, and took care of the business side of things. His ghost made himself known by moving tools used for candy making, tying people's shoes together if they stood still too long, and flinging handfuls of change around the upstairs office, as well as stomping around, and opening and closing doors and drawers. Lights would go on and off, and the radio would turn on when no one was in the office, much to the consternation of the employees downstairs who knew they were alone in the shop. Once Leah was gone, the front of the shop began to be affected, too. Staff would watch in amazement as the lines of Victoria Creams would sort of shuffle side to side, ever so slightly into straighter lines. Employees would slave over a new display window, leave for the day, and when they returned in the morning, they would find the display in a new configuration, apparently one that was more pleasing to Leah. On one occasion, a woman entered the shop and decided to take a sample from a tray. The woman did not like the sample and spat it into a small paper cup. For some reason, she put the cup back on to the tray. As she turned to leave the store, she felt something hit the back of her head. She looked down and saw the sample cup with her chewed up chocolate in it. Someone had thrown it at the back of her head. As she prepared to storm in and demand answers, she noticed that none of the employees had moved. In fact, no one was near the tray. Apparently Leah never could abide rudeness, and the lady's behaviour did not impress her, nor did she find it acceptable.

Noises, sounds, and little tricks still go on, but there were two instances in particular that caused a bit more trouble than the regular occurrences.

After Rogers' Chocolates began producing a milk chocolate line, employees would come into the shop in the mornings to find piles of milk chocolates in heaps on the floor, crushed into mush. In the kitchens, employees would find whole trays tipped off the tables, while the trays of dark chocolates next to them were untouched. Stove burners with milk chocolate tempering on them would turn off. Things got so bad that the shop reached out to local historian and Ghostly Walks proprietor John Adams, who explained that Charles had only ever produced dark chocolate and the change was probably upsetting him. Still perplexed about what to do, the answer came from one of the counter employees. "Just tell him," she said. "Talk out loud and explain the situation." So that's what store managers ended up doing: speaking out loud about the change, telling Charles people enjoyed milk chocolate and that by destroying the trays and disrupting the production, he was actually hurting the business. It must have worked as nothing untoward ever happened to the milk chocolates again.

The second instance happened in December in the early 1980s. Staff noticed a smudged handprint on one of the mirrors that hangs approximately eight feet off the ground at the back of the store. This was unusual, as you would need to get on a ladder or step stool to create the print. When asked, none of the staff had been on any ladders. However, a dutiful staff member climbed onto a small stepladder and cleaned the mirror. The next morning, the print was back, and once again a staff member hauled out the ladder, climbed up, and cleaned the mirror. Unfortunately, every morning the smudged handprint was back. In Victoria, receiving a Rogers' Cream in the toe of your Christmas stocking is a tradition, so things were getting very busy in the shop. The staff did not appreciate these hijinks and they began to get bit snippy with each other as they attempted to find out who was playing this not-so-very-funny-anymore prank. After a couple of weeks, things reached a boiling point and the managers called everyone together and asked them each to climb the ladder, put their hand next to the hand print, and prove that it wasn't them creating this disturbance. One by one, the employees did just that, until one of the last people to climb the ladder said to the group, "Wait a minute, this isn't a smudged print of a perfect hand; this a perfect print of a damaged hand." They looked closer and realized it was true. The handprint resembled something like a lobster claw—a print that would have perfectly matched Freddie's disfigured hand if he had been around to compare it with. A bit of a chill went through the group, but it was rather nice to think that perhaps Freddie had come back to spend one last Christmas with his mother and father in the chocolate shop that brought all of them so much distress in the end.

OLD MORRIS
TOBACCONISTS

THE OLD MORRIS Tobacconists shop, established in 1892, has been in its current location, designed by Thomas Hooper, since 1910. What is significant about the building is the lushness of the materials with which it was built: marble, onyx, and mahogany. These materials reflect the richness of a gentlemen's club from that era, a smart choice at the time because the clientele was predominantly male. There is a beautiful and unique glass canopy over the main door. Another feature that makes the store unique is the electrolier that stands in the centre of the shop. Handmade from rare Mexican onyx, it is the last functioning model of its kind in the world and stands ready to light any cigar presented to it (if it were legal to smoke in public spaces in the city of Victoria).

There have been a number of paranormal investigations at this location, including one done by local paranormal investigator Andrea Bailey, who is the founder of Unearthing Shadows Paranormal. According to Andrea, there had been reports of someone moving around upstairs. Employees knew that there was no one on any other floor, and yet they could hear an office chair rolling around, cupboards and drawers opening and closing, and someone clearing their throat every once in a while. There were also sensations of cold spots and unsettlement in the back of the store.

Andrea went in with her team and began using equipment to try to capture electronic voice phenomena (EVPs), and to see if they could get any readings on electromagnetic field (EMF) readers. Andrea confirms they did pick up some interesting things during their investigation.

While the entity who resides upstairs didn't reveal his identity, he was happy to come forward and communicate. Everyone is quite sure it's a male, possibly an old employee who died upstairs while at work. However, something downstairs is really what caught Andrea's attention. At one time in Victoria, there were rumours of a full underground tunnel system. On some side streets, you will see purple, square blocks in the sidewalk. What's under them now are storerooms, which extend beneath the sidewalks; the blocks are there to provide natural light. When Andrea was downstairs in the tobacconists shop, she found a blocked off passage entrance. Here's what she had to say about what she found:

> There seems to be a man associated with the tunnel. It seems like he may have passed there, maybe not by accident. We had a lot of communication that revolved around a shovel and injury from behind, so we were thinking maybe someone came up behind him and hit him on the head with a shovel. I am not sure he knows what happened to him and it seems like he's maybe reaching out for help. A few of us felt a hand coming through the tunnel that's closed up with rock and mortar, so someone is there.

Employees have experienced poltergeist activity, including items flying off shelves into the middle of the store and light bulbs exploding for no reason. Employees have also complained about feeling watched down in the basement, and hearing sounds down there that have no source. All in all, this building is definitely home to some spirits.

MUNRO'S BOOKS

Now HOME TO one of Canada's premier bookstores, this building used to house a bank. It was designed in 1909, again by our friend Thomas Hooper (who really should be called Victoria's haunted building architect). When the bank moved in 1963, Jim Munro opened a bookshop there. Munro's Books has recently been named the third greatest bookstore in the world. During its years as a bank, however, the building saw a bit of a darker history.

A young woman who worked at the bank had been slowly and steadily embezzling from the bank. Unfortunately for her, she was caught. The bank did not let on that it knew and simply called the police. When the police walked into the bank, the young woman knew right away why they were there and ran to the back room. A gun was stored in the back in case it was needed to protect the money. She barricaded herself in the room and, despite the police entreating her to come out, took her own life.

That back room is accessible by a door in the rear of the building, where there is a covered parking garage. On rainy, late-night ghost tours, we will often go into the garage to tell stories rather than stand out in the rain. One night, a good friend of mine, Aaron, was on the tour and was listening to the story. The shop had been closed for hours and no one was in the building. He quietly knocked on the door three times. To his great shock, three knocks answered back. Aaron looked at his mom, who had accompanied him on the tour, and asked, "Did you hear that?" His mom said she had. Aaron knocked twice, and the entity responded by duplicating his knock. At that point the tour moved on, but ever since, Aaron has been a believer.

There have also been reports of books coming off shelves; sometimes it seems in response to what people are looking for. One woman with whom I spoke, Cecilia, had been searching for a particular cookbook that her mother wanted, and she couldn't find it anywhere. Cecilia went to Munro's with her friend. As they headed for the cookbook section, she mentioned to her friend that if she could just find this particular book, she would be so happy as she'd been looking for so long. They arrived in the cookbook section, and looked on in amazement as a book seemed to gently ease itself off a lower shelf and fall to the floor. It was the exact cookbook Cecilia had been searching for.

There have been other reports of books coming off shelves, but from what I hear they were more random, or to get attention. There may be other reports of ghostly customer service happening, but Cecilia's is certainly the most compelling to date.

MURCHIE'S TEA & COFFEE

THIS VICTORIA STAPLE is actually an import from New Westminster in the Lower Mainland. John Murchie was a Scottish immigrant who started his life in tea by delivering tea to Queen Victoria while working for a tea company in England. John started his own company in Canada in 1894, and the company has never looked back. The building in which they conduct business in Victoria has had some ghostly activity over the years. The front part of the building seems to be unaffected, but the back of Murchie's is a different story. There have been persistent reports by the after-hours security staff as well as a member of the Murchie's staff of footsteps up and down the stairs; even when the store is closed and the building is relatively empty, the elevator is called by an unseen presence and travels between floors in what appears to be a random pattern. In the shop on the left-hand side of the establishment, things have come off shelves and broken, and not only at the hands of clumsy tourists. Sometimes they fall completely on their own. People have also reported hearing doors slam heavily in the lower level when everything is locked up and no one is supposed to be down there.

I have been in Murchie's more than once but I have never felt comfortable there. In the back room of the café, on the right-hand side of the building, you will often see people enjoying the various baked goods, sandwiches, cakes, and of course the varied and famous tea. However, I never see anyone relaxed in there, just lingering on their own. It's mostly tourists and family groups in that section of the café, and no one seems to go in there to unwind. After spending some time in there, I can understand why. I couldn't tell you who is in the back part of the building and enjoys making noise, but there is definitely someone there who doesn't want to let go of their small haunted area of Murchie's café.

THE GUILD

T HE BUILDING ON Wharf Street that houses this restaurant has been a number of things in its past. It was originally a warehouse in the late 1800s serving the wharf. It is known for having a huge whale mural on one side of it, but it is also known for having more than one ghost story emerge from within its walls.

Even before I knew this building had a history, I remember going there in 2007 when it was another restaurant. My wife and I shared a meal and I went downstairs to use the restroom. The lower I got, the more uncomfortable I felt. I went into the bathroom and had to keep turning around because I was genuinely convinced someone was in there with me. I couldn't wait to get out. I practically backed out of the bathroom and then bolted up the stairs, feeling a little foolish. Now that I have heard some of the other stories and talked to some of the people who currently work there, I don't feel as foolish.

The story of an experience a young woman had while attending a Chinese medicine school that was located in the basement level of the building has stuck around. The young lady was heading to the school for a class. As there are some colourful characters who hang around the park beside the building, the school had a protocol: each student was given a key to enter the building through the creepy steel door at the side. Once through the door, they were instructed to lock it behind them, and then open the second door to go down the long dark hallway toward the classroom at the end of the hall. As this student went in the first door, she turned to lock it behind her. Once this was accomplished, she opened the second door, but as she did, she felt a large bulky male presence push past her and hurry down the hall. She could see him framed in the light from the classroom at the end of the hall. The lights in the hallway were off and the switch was halfway down the long hall. As she moved toward the switch, she could see the man going down the hall and began calling out to him. "Excuse me, I'm sorry, what are you doing? You're not supposed to be here." She finally reached the switch, but when she turned on the light, the outline of the man disappeared. At this point, she was very upset and made her way to the classroom, where she quickly relayed what had just happened. As she did, she saw that other students were nodding their heads as if they had had the same experience. The instructors took it seriously and one of the Feng Shui masters created a large poster-sized set of gold characters that were believed to ward off evil. It didn't do everything they had hoped for, and the school soon moved.

I was able to speak to a number of the servers at what is now the Guild. They have had a startlingly high number of experiences in the building. One woman, Laura, told me she often hears someone walking around in the back staircase. Laura knows it is a male presence, and she often hears him ascending and descending the stairs when she is the only one in the restaurant. One of her most upsetting moments back there was when she walked into the stairway and happened to look up. She saw a man hanging from the landing, as if he had committed suicide. She backed out of the stairwell, and now avoids it as best she can. While she still hears the footsteps, she has never seen the hanged man again.

Another server, Julia, had a unique experience. One night she was waiting for a group to leave and actually fell asleep in the upper room they use for private parties. Unbeknownst to her, when she awoke it was three AM. Not only had the group left, but the restaurant was shut and locked down. No one else was in the building. It appeared the other staff had forgotten she was up there. As she struggled to wake up, she could hear voices downstairs, all male. "Oh no," she thought, "they're still here?" Julia figured she had better get down stairs or they might never leave. She reached the top of the stairs and realized that all of the lights were out. When she walked down the stairs, she knew then that it was much later than she had thought and the restaurant was in fact empty. The voices continued, loud enough to be heard, but not loud enough to be distinct. Julia began walking toward the back of the restaurant where she heard the voices, but just before she reached the back, the voices stopped. By this time—it felt to her like hours had passed rather than minutes—she knew something strange was going on, so she got out of there as quickly as possible. At other times she has felt extremely uncomfortable in the basement storeroom, an experience she shares with the other servers.

The last server with whom I spoke shared a few of the same experiences. But along with the fear of the storeroom, the sounds of someone climbing up and down the stairs, and customers complaining to her about feeling watched or uncomfortable downstairs where the washrooms are, Carrie had her own unusual experience in the building. One night after the restaurant closed, she was rolling cutlery into napkins for the next day. She was alone in the dining room area and became aware of a presence beside her, watching what she was doing with interest. Carrie didn't look up, but saw in her peripheral vision that it was a man in a black blazer. She could see the stitching on the arms as he was standing quite near her. When she looked up, no one was there. There is no doubt in her mind about what she saw. She believes that her place of employment not only serves great food, but it is also profoundly haunted.

When I went there with Dawn Kirkham, founder of Beyond Belief Paranormal, we shared some appetizers and spoke of what we felt in the restaurant. Dawn picked up on a formally dressed male who was leaning in and very interested in our conversation. She also picked up on a female presence who was dressed as if she worked in a shop in the early 1900s. I looked up at the wall beside our table and there was a picture of the building. It had been home to a retail establishment at one time, so it was nice to see some confirmation. Neither of the presences were particularly intrusive, but they were both there and fascinated with what was going on. Dawn and I agreed that the Guild is definitely home to more than one spirit.

THE KEG

THIS RESTAURANT IS housed in one of the oldest buildings in Victoria. It was built right beside the front gate of the old Fort Victoria. One interesting thing about the Keg chain of restaurants is that no matter what city they are in, they always seem to pick haunted old buildings for their locations.

The restaurant at the corner of Wharf and Fort Streets certainly had some ghostly issues before undergoing renovations in the early 2000s—shadow people in the kitchen, perfectly set tables being messed up, and unexplained noises in an otherwise empty restaurant were pretty standard experiences for the staff at the Keg—but once the renovations started, it riled up whatever entities were in there.

Renovations or major changes to any building seem to lead to increased activity in the spirit world. No one is sure why, but it may be because spirits dislike change of any kind. Perhaps it's because they don't understand what's going on.

A friend of mine once started some major renovations on her house. She was aware that she shared her home with some spirits, but they generally got along. As the renovations progressed, the entities became more and more agitated and began doing things that were disruptive and even a bit dangerous, such as turning the stove up to maximum when she was cooking dinner, hiding car keys, slamming doors in the middle of the night, and scaring the cat and dog. Soon they were messing with the contractors' tools and causing so many disturbances that the contractors refused to stay in the building. For the first (and so far the last) time, she addressed the ghosts and said out loud: "Look, I know you're not happy with the work that's going on here, but this house needs to be changed to suit the family. If you keep up with this foolishness, we will have to sell it and then who knows who you will get in here. So, let's agree that you will stop all of this activity, we will finish the renovations as quickly as possible, and then we can all go back to normal." She then left the house and went to the store. When she came back, she said the house felt calmer and she was much more relaxed. The renovations continued on without a problem and things settled into the normal routines with the occasional bump and thump every once in a while.

The good people running the Keg unfortunately were granted no such respite. As renovations on the restaurant continued, the spirit activity ramped up. More shadow figures were seen, and not just in the kitchen anymore; they were also seen in the restaurant dining room. Things in the kitchen came off the shelves; the pots hanging on racks clanked together when there was nothing to move them. In one case, a full wine glass shattered spontaneously at a table. (The servers moved the startled couple to a new table without admitting anything unusual had happened.) Glasses would move around on their own, and set tables weren't just messed up: cutlery and napkins from place settings were found under the tables that they were supposed to be on. One of the most upsetting things for the customers was getting locked in the bathrooms when there wasn't even a way to lock the bathroom door. The door would just stick closed. No amount of hauling on it would move the door until whatever was holding it closed decided to let go.

Once the renovation was over, things seemed to settle down again—well, as settled as they get. They still see shadow people passing through the kitchen, which was built directly in the original gateway of the old fort. The shadow people don't seem interested in what's going on around them; they're just spirits going about their day.

No one in the service industry seems too bothered about the ghosts that haunt Victoria's restaurants. Most of them have at least one story to tell, but it's generally understood that we share the buildings we use today with those who came before us. It's so common downtown that it isn't that big of a deal, but it is great news if you're into ghosts.

FAN TAN ALLEY

THE RICH STORY of Fan Tan Alley is about gambling, prostitution, drugs, and eluding the police. It is also about love, hate, betrayal, and murder. The only thing it's missing is rock 'n' roll.

Fan Tan Alley is officially the narrowest street in Canada. It was designated as a heritage property by the City of Victoria in 2001. It is a significant part of Victoria's Chinatown—one of the oldest Chinatowns in Canada. Victoria's Chinatown was born out of the Fraser Canyon Gold Rush in 1858. Thousands of Chinese immigrants came to British Columbia expecting to strike it rich. But like many other gold rush hopefuls, most did not, and many Chinese immigrants ended up in Victoria.

The original purpose of Fan Tan Alley, which runs between Fisgard Street and Pandora Avenue, was pretty straightforward. Gambling-den owners were looking for an answer to the question of how to grant access to gambling, opium, and prostitutes, but provide limited entrance to law enforcement. Their solution was an alley so narrow that only one or perhaps two people could enter it at a time. As you walk down the alley, you see doorways on either side, which in those days led to passages that cut through the buildings to grant you access to any vice you were looking for. These passages had multiple doors and turn-offs. The alley itself had wooden gates at either end and gatekeepers decided who was allowed in and who wasn't. At the first hint of trouble, individual gambling dens could be secured; patrons and staff could be hidden away or hustled out alternative exits through the buildings quickly and effectively.

Now, the illicit gambling dens are all gone from Fan Tan Alley, but there is still a resident from that time making his presence known. He is not a spirit that sits still. He runs fast and without regard for anyone in his way. The spirit of Chung is still running for his life.

This story begins in May 1889. Chung was a seventeen-year-old boy who spent a great deal of time in Chinatown. He worked as a servant in a hotel, where he had a small room, a few blocks away from Fan Tan Alley. On one of his trips through Chinatown, he happened upon a young woman named Yau (Yow).

Yau was not just any young woman. She was the most beautiful woman in all of Chinatown. Her owner, and yes, I mean owner, Yip Tang, had purchased her in San Francisco. He paid a huge sum of money for her. Anyone who met her would have agreed that it was a bargain price, no matter the sum. Yau was brought to Victoria for one purpose: to be a human advertisement for Yip Tang's brothel. Yau's job was to sit in the lower window of the brothel, also referred to as a sing-song girl house, and try to tempt men in. She would converse flirtatiously with and sing to the men she saw on the street. Yau was not only stunningly beautiful, she was also the best singer, the greatest conversationalist, and she spoke several languages fluently. In essence, Yau's job was to get attention. Once she had their attention, she would invite the men who she had enchanted into the house to meet her sisters. As a sing-song girl, she had it pretty good: she didn't have to entertain gentlemen one-on-one on a regular basis; she was the window dressing to sell the goods inside. Yau was clothed in beautiful gowns and fed the finest meals, and she genuinely enjoyed talking to people and performing her songs for admiring audiences.

Unfortunately for the shy and gentle Chung, no one had filled him in on how sing-song girls or brothels were supposed to work. When Yau began to talk to him, flirt with him, and pay more attention to him than any other woman ever had, he fell deeply, madly, and truly in love with her. He believed she must feel the same way about him because of the attention she lavished on him.

What happens when there's a teenage boy and a pretty girl? Usually a great big glass of stupid. Unfortunately for Chung, stupid is exactly what he became when it came to Yau.

Chung came up with a rather ridiculous plan. As he passed Yau's window, she greeted him with a smile and a flirtatious wink as usual, but rather than bask in her beauty and make small talk, he revealed his passion. Chung stood in front of the window and boldly declared his love for Yau. He asserted he knew she felt the same way about him. Then he approached the window and asked her to marry him. He promised they would leave Victoria, go to Vancouver, and make a new life together. Yau did the best she could to explain that it would never be possible: Yip Tang would never let her go. She had to decline his offer. Surely Yau would have dealt with this sort of situation before, and surely this same explanation had been sufficient, with no one getting their feelings hurt. This time, however, it did not work. Yau had gravely miscalculated Chung's feelings for her and the passion he was sure they shared.

Chung returned the next day and Yau greeted him as warmly as ever, thinking that their situation was plain to Chung. He approached the window and put a small vial of poison into her hand. Chung told Yau that all she needed to do was put it into Yip

Tang's food and he would die. Then they would be able to run off together and be married and happy. The thoughts that must have gone through poor Yau's mind! At this point, her professional veneer cracked. She must have been a bit frightened by this young man who was willing to kill to be with her. She began shouting at him in the street: "No! Why would I ever go with you, a poor, penniless servant boy? Do you not see all I have here, the food I eat, the clothes I wear? Even if I were free to marry, I would still never choose you. Go away and *never* come back to my window again!" Yau closed the shutters and slammed the window shut.

Chung was shocked and deeply humiliated. He had been shamed in the street. Soon everyone would know of his rejection and failure. It was more than he could bear so he cooked up a rather gruesome plan to regain his honour.

Chung had a friend who worked in a fish processing plant. He convinced his young friend that although Yau had rejected him, all she really needed was a chance to talk to him away from Yip Tang to see how much she loved him. Then she would be willing to marry him. He told his friend that all he needed to do was distract Yau because she would not speak to Chung. When she was distracted, Chung and his friend would grab her, pull her out the window, and take her to one of the dock buildings so Chung could convince her to marry him. Obviously Chung's friend must have been quite young and naive to agree to help Chung win over his lady. Kidnapping is never a good way to show the object of your affection you are serious about them. This was, even without what happened later on, a terrible plan.

Chung stood around the corner of the brothel as his friend began to talk to Yau. She was as enchanting as ever and his friend made sure he stood off to the side so she couldn't see Chung approaching. When Chung reached Yau, he grabbed hold of her hair and pulled her out of the window. But then, much to the shock of Yau and Chung's friend, Chung pulled out a sharp curved fish knife. In one powerful motion, he cut off Yau's head.

As this happened, everyone in the alley froze in shock. The sound of Yau's blood spattering thickly onto the sidewalk punctuated the silence, and Chung dropped Yau's head with a sickening thump. Then he dropped the knife and began to run before anyone else could react.

Chung reached the entrance to Fan Tan Alley as people began to pursue him. He ran as fast as he could, pushing, shoving, and running, anything he could do to get past anyone else in the alley. Chung kept running until he got to the hotel where he worked, and slipped into the basement. The other people who worked there saw him go into the basement, but didn't give the action much thought; after all Chung belonged there. But it didn't take long for posters to go up with Chung's face on them. Yip Tang was offering a 150 dollar reward—equivalent to more than 3,500 dollars today—for Chung's arrest. A witness at the hotel came forward and soon afterward the police arrived to search it. They looked through all of the rooms, in cupboards, under beds, everywhere. They had just about given up when they poked their lanterns into the room where the coal was stored in the hotel. They didn't see anything and went to leave, but, on a hunch, one officer turned around at the last minute and his light caught the whites of Chung's eyes, which he had opened thinking he was safe.

Chung was quickly arrested and taken to jail; the outcome of his trial was not in question. There were dozens of witnesses who had seen him commit the horrific crime. When he was arrested, his clothes were still stiff and caked in Yau's blood. Chung knew what his future held. He decided to speed up the process. He hanged himself in his dark prison cell using his own shirt and the pipe above his head.

The jailers, not being familiar with and probably not even caring about Chinese burial customs, dug Chung a pauper's grave and dumped his body in it. The proper way to send someone onto the next life in Chinese culture is with offerings of food, money, and large gongs to provide for the next life and ensure that the spirit knows it is supposed to move on. This would have been doubly important in the case of Chung as no one wanted the ghost of a murderer hanging around.

It appears Chung was well aware of the missed burial rites as things soon became quite unmanageable both at the hotel where he had worked and in Fan Tan Alley. At the hotel, things became so bad that all of the Chinese workers refused to go in. They said they could feel Chung stepping on their heels, watching them, tugging their hair, and tormenting them. The hotel owner was beside himself so he gave them permission to do the rituals that should have accompanied Chung's burial. Things did settle down some after that. As they learned, by leaving small offerings of food out for Chung on a regular basis, they were spared his fits of anger. When he was angry, people would come in to the kitchen to find food dumped out on the floor, knives spinning off work counters, and stoves either turned up to high or turned off altogether. These things have continued to happen in the kitchens of the restaurants that have been in the space since. Why should the new occupants believe that a century-old ghost would bother them? But once they come in and find the refrigerator door ajar, meals burning, nothing being where it was left, and that horrible feeling of someone being right behind them as they work, they quickly leave out some fruit and a small glass of beer to appease the spirit of Chung, who still thinks he works at the hotel. It does work; the mayhem generally subsides, but the presence never truly goes away.

As for Fan Tan Alley, Chung is still very active there. You may feel like you've stumbled or tripped and hit your shoulder into the red brick buildings that line the alley. You may feel a very strong wind come whipping down the alley, even though the air is still. Some even hear the clatter of Chung's feet as he tries to race for freedom and escape his crime, or they feel his hands as Chung pushes them out of the way. Other people have reported feeling watched as they make their way down the alley. Once on a Ghostly Walks tour, after the guide recounted Chung's story, he noticed a woman who looked shaken and then relieved. She told the guide afterward she had heard and seen a young Chinese man with stained clothing running toward her; she had even pressed herself up against the wall to get out of his way. Though no one else had seen anything, the woman was thankful to have heard the story, because the experience now made sense.

As for Yau, her owner Yip Tang obviously felt great affection for her. Yau's funeral was one of the largest and grandest that the city of Victoria had ever seen. It must have been very grand indeed for there have been no reports of Yau remaining behind, so her soul must have truly moved on to the next destination.

I have been in both locations where Chung is said to reside. Even before I heard the story about Fan Tan Alley I felt very uncomfortable there. It may be because it's so narrow that I felt closed in. I'm not sure. I do know that when I go down there now, and I often do, it's with more understanding of who may still be there, so I don't feel any fear.

As for the restaurant, there's a presence there to be sure, but it's not angry and murderous. In fact, I'm not even sure Chung realizes that he's dead or that the original hotel that he worked in is no longer there, and so he still behaves as he always has in his spirit form (though now that offices have replaced the hotel on the floors above the restaurant, I have to wonder what Chung does to keep busy). The restaurant still leaves out a small offering of food and drink for him, and his spirit remains relatively calm. While you may not notice a presence in the restaurant, go down Fan Tan Alley if you can. It's definitely worth the brush with history, if not a ghost.

THE CHRIST CHURCH CATHEDRAL PRECINCT

PIONEER SQUARE, OR
THE OLD BURYING GROUNDS

ESTABLISHED IN 1855, Pioneer Square was used as a cemetery until 1873. At that point, it had over 1,300 permanent residents buriedbelow its surface, and the city established a new and much larger cemetery in Ross Bay. The old burying grounds were the second graveyard to be used by Victorians. The first graveyard was set up rather casually when Fort Victoria was established. It was at the corner of what is now Douglas and Johnson Streets. The problem with that graveyard was that the land was waterlogged clay, so whenever the weather was even remotely damp or rainy, which was most of the time between September and April, the graves would fill up with water and the coffins would burst to the surface. The early Victorians got around this by having not only grave diggers at the funerals ready to fill in the dirt, but also men with spear-like poles, who, after all the mourners and families had left the site, would punch holes into the coffins so they could fill with water and hopefully not re-emerge later. Obviously with the population increasing and the rather unpleasant side effect of the graveyard, the city needed a solution, and so a new cemetery was established. The Pioneer Square location made much more sense because it was quite a bit higher in elevation and had the added benefit of not having its residents re-emerge in rainy weather. Pioneer Square was actually the home base for one of Victoria's very first documented ghosts.

Adelaide Griffin was co-owner of the Boomerang Saloon in Bastion Square, until she died in a typhoid epidemic in 1861. After her death, she was frequently seen in Bastion Square, and she became famous for being the Ghost of Langley Street in downtown Victoria, near where her saloon was located. At one time in Victoria's history, Adelaide was seen so frequently that spotting her ghost was actually a popular activity. Going downtown to spot the Ghost of Langley Street filled up more than a few weekend nights for Victoria's youth.

Another famous ghost that lingers in the former graveyard is that of Robert Johnson. Johnson was one of Victoria's founding fathers who took his own life with a barber's razor. He has been known to appear in front of people in Pioneer Square with a blade in his hands, which he drags across his throat, disturbing the restful vistas you're hoping to see as you relax in the park.

Other people visiting the park have reported hearing voices call out to them, lights floating at night, and the feeling that they're being watched. I know whenever I have cut through the park, I have felt very uncomfortable, like I'm in some kind of danger, but can't really pinpoint why. There is a sense of uneasiness there. I suppose I thought they'd moved all of the bodies to the Ross Bay Cemetery, but as it happens, they did not. Those left behind are still very much interested in not resting in their final resting place.

CATHEDRAL HALL/CHRIST CHURCH CATHEDRAL SCHOOL

WORKED IN THE Christ Church Cathedral precinct for almost nine years. During that time, I had plenty of reasons to be all throughout the buildings, so I thought I'd share a few of the experiences I had while working there.

I had many opportunities to be in the Cathedral Hall and Christ Church Cathedral School. I helped out with youth events there, and my son went to school there. When we had events in the hall, we knew we were the only ones there and the custodians would lock us in the building so no one else could wander in. The other leader and I would be down on the main floor and we would hear noises upstairs: furniture moving around, footsteps, doors opening and closing. One particularly memorable time, we were at the school about an hour early so we could set up. My co-leader and I were in the building alone. We distinctly heard a door close on the level above us and looked at each other.

"That's weird," I said. "I thought we were the only ones here?"

"We are. I spoke to the custodian before he left and he said he would be back at 9:30 PM when we were all done."

"Oh," was all I could muster in reply.

We decided we'd better go check it out, as we were expecting a rather large group of teenagers and didn't want to catch someone who might be working upstairs unaware. We headed up to the second floor and began walking along a classroom-lined corridor. We didn't see any lights on in the classrooms, nor did we see anyone through the classroom door windows as we moved slowly along the hallway.

We reached the end of the hall and looked at each other.

"There's no one up here," I needlessly stated.

"Yeah, I see that. It's really strange," he replied.

As we began to move back down the hall, we heard the distinct sound of a door banging closed. The door was to the last classroom on the right; it was the door we had just been standing next to, discussing how the school was indeed vacant.

Being the brave, lion-hearted soul that I am, I yipped like a small dog and ran. I may have even used my co-leader for traction by shoving him toward the sound as I bolted in panic. The combination of that echoing bang and the knowledge that no living person was up there with us was enough to send me running—it was not my finest hour.

After that incident, whenever we were running an event and heard footsteps, doors closing, and chairs being moved, we ignored it. Occasionally, one of the teens would ask what the noise was or who was upstairs. Regardless of the noise or the time, we both automatically answered, "The custodian." The church hall just feels like a place of shadows. I've been there during the day and I think whatever is in there goes dormant when it's full of children and energy. But once it's quiet, dark, and lonely, the presence becomes more active. I wouldn't even go to the bathroom in that building, I was so spooked. And I always made sure I was never, ever the last one out.

THE DEANERY

UILT IN 1938, this lovely house was originally the home of the dean; it is now the cathedral offices. As I worked in the diocesan offices, merely a parking lot away, I had many occasions to be in this building as well. This home has its own energy that is different from the rest of the precinct. I can't explain why it's so different, but it definitely is. When I was downstairs, I would often hear noises upstairs. The noises were the usual footsteps and doors closing, but softly. There is a stately presence that remains here.

Once when I was upstairs, I was walking down the hall, looking down, and I felt like I had just run into someone. Looking up, I said, "Oh, excuse me." But there was no one there. There was no one else in the hall. I felt like an idiot.

There never seemed to be anything really scary in the deanery. It was a very mild presence, but it was a presence nonetheless. I never did any research into who it might be as there didn't seem to be a need. As I have mentioned, I don't go looking for this kind of thing, so if something is there and it's cool with me being around, I'm not going to push too hard to figure anything else out. I definitely got the feeling that it was a female spirit and she was just happy to be there. She liked things to be done properly and enjoyed having people around. It is quite unusual for a spirit to be so relaxed actually, but this one seemed happy enough. My best guess is that it was the spirit of a former dean's wife who loved the place as if it were her own, and even though it never was truly hers, she couldn't bear to leave.

BISHOP'S CHAPEL/
DIOCESAN OFFICE

THIS GHOSTLY EXPERIENCE was my first one in Victoria. When I began working for the diocese, I also helped out with some of the cleaning around our office. I'd go in at night when it was quiet and there was no one around to get in the way. The bishop's chapel doubles as the diocesan archives as well as a small chapel. My first time going into the chapel was pretty dramatic, much more dramatic and sudden than any other experience I've ever had. Usually there's a bit of a build up to something happening, but not this time. I unlocked the door, lugging the vacuum cleaner with me. I needed to empty the garbage cans, vacuum, dust, and clean the one tiny bathroom. It wasn't really a burden, but the work needed to be done.

As soon as I got through the door, I knew something was off. I flipped on the lights, but they didn't seem to be very bright, and even though it was a warm late summer day outside, it was icy cold inside the chapel.

I decided to ignore the weirdness if I could, and just do what I had to do so I could get out of there quickly. I plugged the vacuum in and began cleaning the rugs. Then I decided I should empty the garbage cans first. I turned off the vacuum and emptied the garbage can in the room with me into a big bag, and then made my way through the door at the end of the chapel to the addition that had been built to house the archives. The doors didn't quite match up, so if you were in the bathroom area, you couldn't see the rest of the chapel.

As I emptied out the garbage in the archives, I thought I heard something in the chapel, but figured it was nothing. When I came back out, however, I was more than a little surprised. The vacuum cleaner plug had been pulled out of the wall. It was not just resting beside the wall, but rather it looked like it had been grabbed and thrown toward the vacuum itself because it was lying in the middle of the floor.

Okay, that's sort of odd, I thought. I plugged the cord back in, still feeling the heavy and almost angry presence in the small space with me, and continued to clean the rugs. When I was done, I decided to clean the bathroom before I dusted. I unplugged the vacuum myself this time, determined not to let *that* happen again, and went into the bathroom. While I was in the bathroom, I once again heard noises out in the main chapel. I wasn't overly anxious to check them out. Eventually, though, I ran out of reasons to stay in the tiny bathroom and made my way back into the chapel.

What I found there did not make me happy. Three of the four chairs that were in the chapel were on their backs. They looked as if they'd been casually tipped over. Of course, I knew they'd been perfectly upright when I went into the bathroom, so it was really hard to deny that something odd was going on.

This is when I figured I'd better just stop and feel out what was happening. I lowered my guard and tried to get a sense of the presence. I felt the mood shift very slightly and it became less hostile. It also drew me to a plaque on wall.

The plaque explained why the chapel had been built. A young man by the name of John Yarrow had died while at Cambridge University in 1938. His mother had the chapel built in his honour in 1939 and gifted it to the diocese. Could a young man who had died in another country really have been brought back to his homeland? Was it his spirit hanging around in a chapel built in his memory? I figured it was worth at least asking some questions. Out loud I said, "John, I'm not here to bother you or disturb you, I'm just here to keep this place looking nice. As this is your chapel, I would think you would want that. Okay?"

Of course, I didn't get a response, for which I am grateful, but it did seem like the whole building relaxed just a little. As I left, I said, "Bye, John, see you next week." Then I locked the door behind me and went on my way.

The next week, I opened the door and said, "Hello, John, just me, here to tidy up." And flicked on the lights and got to work. Other than a box of paper clips falling from a desk and hitting the floor while I was cleaning the bathroom, nothing much happened. As before, when I was done, I said goodbye to John as I locked the door behind me.

Over the next weeks and months, the feeling in the chapel changed. It was no longer angry; it was almost expectant. The lights were brighter, although it was always colder in there than anywhere else. One day while I was cleaning, I was suddenly compelled to sing old hymns. I just started singing out loud "How Great Thou Art" and "The Old Rugged Cross" and "Just As I Am" while I cleaned and worked. The acoustics were pretty awesome in the chapel, so I sounded good. When I was singing, the mood lightened even more, almost to the point where it felt happy, contented, and joyful in the chapel. So that became my routine. I would always say hello as I entered, sing some old hymns, and then say goodbye as I left. I never had anything strange happen again, and I never felt threatened or afraid in that building either.

My office was in the basement of the diocesan office, where the leadership of the diocese conducts business. When I was there on my own, some strange things would happen. I seemed to hear footsteps all the time. If I was alone in the office, the perimeter alarm would be on, so I could hear if anyone came into the building. But when I was in my basement office, I would often hear someone walking around on the main floor. If I happened to be on the main floor, I'd hear footsteps on the second level, and if I was up on the second level, I'd hear the same sound of someone walking on the main floor.

At first I didn't mention the footsteps to anyone, but eventually I summoned my courage and asked another employee who was often in the building alone whether she had ever experienced anything unusual. She looked at me for a half second and then said, "The footsteps?" I was amazed and, quite frankly, relieved to know I wasn't the only one hearing the footsteps. I did some research, and I think I may have figured out to whom the footsteps belonged.

The site of the diocesan office was originally the space for the bishop's palace, the home where the bishop would have lived. It had been torn down and a new building erected in its place in 1994. One of the last bishops to live there had a wife who was agoraphobic and hadn't left the home in nearly nineteen years. Apparently she remained on the second floor and never came downstairs, allowing the servants to look after her. I suppose you can take the building away from the ghost, but you can't take the ghost away from the building.

I never felt fearful there, except for one time. The diocesan office had been built on the original stone foundation for the bishop's palace. Half of the basement had been turned into cement-encased platforms, which were used for storage, and it was never an overwhelmingly welcoming space. But I didn't mind working down there as long as the door to the storage area remained closed, and, as foolish as it sounds, I never sat with my back to that door. One afternoon the office was closed, but I needed to catch up on some work, so I went in, locking the door behind me. I hadn't been there more than an hour when I had the overwhelming feeling that something dark was not happy that I was there. This was not an "Ooooh, I feel creepy" type of feeling; it was more like being threatened, yelled at, and ordered out at the same time. I packed up and left.

I still don't know what I encountered that day. Maybe it was a presence used to having its alone time, maybe it was just passing through. Either way, I never sensed it again.

OUTSIDE OF DOWNTOWN

THE DELTA OCEAN
POINTE RESORT

IT WAS A dark and stormy night—no really, it was. On the night of September 22, 1899, the rain and the wind were lashing the windows of the Pilgrim Bakery, situated at the foot of Johnson and Wharf Streets. And the owner of the bakery, forty-four-year-old Agnes Bing, was about to make a terrible choice.

Agnes was unusual for her time, as she owned her own bakery when most women did not own businesses of any kind. Her husband had given her permission to do this, because he suffered from what was known then as paralytic fever. Since he couldn't work, Agnes knew it was up to her to ensure that her family had the things that most families enjoy, like food and shelter, so she started the bakery. While it was not high class, it did a steady trade with the dubious businesses and patrons that surrounded it.

Lower Johnson Street in the late 1800s was not the best neighbourhood to frequent, unless you were looking for wine, women, and song. There were more saloons and houses of ill repute in that small section of town than there were buildings. Often there was more than one saloon per building, each on a separate floor. As for houses with overly affectionate young women, there were plenty of those as well. Lower Johnson Street was a loud, wild place in those days, but even people dedicated to the party life enjoy the odd sandwich or cookie now and then.

When Agnes finished work, she usually had three options to get her to her home in Victoria West: take the streetcar that ran across the harbour (the option her husband insisted she take), walk across the Point Ellice Bridge, or walk across the train bridge. On September 22, Agnes unfortunately finished work too late to take the streetcar. This left her with the two other options. Agnes could head out in the wind and the rain and walk up to the streetcar bridge, where she would be able to walk across. It was a good five-block walk just to get to the bridge, which incidentally had hand rails and a place for pedestrians, and then she'd have to double back toward her house on the other side. Not the most enticing option on a cold, rainy night. The final option was to set out over the rail bridge directly across from the bakery, which is now the Johnson Street Bridge. The problem was that the train bridge was literally just rail ties and tracks. There was no walkway, no railing, and no safety measures of any kind. The only way we know that Agnes took the rail bridge is because that is what witnesses told the police early the next day.

As I'm sure you have guessed by now, Agnes never returned home and this story does not have a happy ending, but then, what ghost story does? Her husband, waking in the middle of the night, realized she wasn't there and immediately summoned the police. Even though Agnes's bakery was in a not-very-reputable part of town, the police took her husband's concerns seriously because Agnes ran one of the few legitimate businesses in that area. They immediately canvassed the neighbourhood, asking if anyone had seen Agnes or knew where she might have ended up. One witness mentioned seeing Agnes setting off across the railroad bridge late in the night.

The police were used to seeing bodies off the side of the bridge; it was not uncommon for a sailor who had consumed one too many drinks to attempt to walk back to the naval base over the railroad bridge. Many of them would fall in, and the police would venture out with safety lines to see if they could find a body floating underneath, which they would then hook out with long poles. That's what they started doing for Agnes. They looked across the bridge, waving their lanterns because it was still dark enough to need them, but they didn't see anything below.

Once the police had made it all the way across the bridge, they began to look in the area of the rail yards. I don't know if you have much experience with rail yards, but good things seldom happen to people who wander around them alone. The police began to fan out across the rail yards, looking behind shrubs and trains. Eventually one officer noticed a large number of crows sitting up in a tree making a lot of noise. The crows were circling down toward an object on the ground, and then flying back up. In the police business, they call this a clue, and so the officer ventured forth.

What the officer discovered was one of the most gruesome murders in Victoria's history. He found Agnes lying face up. She had been cut open from sternum to pubic bone and split in half. She had been disembowelled, and her internal organs had been carefully placed around her body in a pattern. When the police told the newspapers what had happened, the papers responded in their usual mature and responsible way by immediately hitting the panic button. The headlines proclaimed things like "Devious fiend loose in Victoria" and "The Ripper in the New World." These weren't completely unfounded ideas as Jack the Ripper had stopped killing only eleven years earlier in London and no one had ever been charged with those crimes. There is, in fact, a widely held belief that the Ripper did escape to the New World and continued his life of crime in a place with less law enforcement, fewer traceable people, and not as much awareness of dangerous men.

As a result of these headlines, Victoria's citizens flew into a panic. For well over a month, women did not go out alone after dark. The police, stumped for any leads, brought in a psychic. Unfortunately, the psychic turned out to be less than helpful and in fact told the media that "he did it once and he will do it again." Naturally the newspapers gleefully shared this psychic tidbit about the killer's intentions, as it was guaranteed to sell many copies.

However, no one was ever charged with this brutal crime. The years went by and the railway yard became smaller and not as frequently used. The yard had originally been surrounded by a First Nations village. As Victoria grew, the city founders appropriated the land from the Aboriginal people and began to develop it. Condominium buildings went up and then the Ocean Pointe Resort was built in the early 1990s. The tradespeople who were building the hotel noticed that strange things were happening in the lobby of the big building. The batteries in power tools would go dead; the workers would experience feelings of panic and fear, and their heart rates would elevate. As soon as they moved out of this one position in the lobby, they felt okay. They didn't talk about it that much as that's not really part of the culture of tradespeople. They are generally focused on working hard and getting the job done.

When the hotel was finally complete, there was a large ribbon-cutting opening ceremony. The ceremony was typical of its type. Plenty of Very Important People, oversized scissors, crustless sandwiches, and much smiling and handshaking. However, there was a curious thing that was a little out of the norm. One of the parties, a gentleman who was on the stage with the Very Important People, noted that even though the lobby was full of people, there was one area of about fifteen square feet that no one was standing in. In fact, the people who were closest to the area could be seen edging away from the perimeter. The gentleman thought this strange, as every other part of the lobby was full of people for the grand opening.

Time has passed and while there have been renovations, that area in the lobby still has a strange effect. However, now it's not power tools that are affected anymore, it's cellphone batteries that inexplicably drain, even though they were full when brought into the hotel. There also remain the feelings of panic, fear, and anxiety, which, sadly, likely mirror the last moments of Agnes's life.

The fact that this hotel is haunted would really not be much of a shock to anyone who had lived in Victoria at that time. Soon after Agnes's death in 1899, a grey lady could be observed across the harbour, wandering around at the edge of the water, close to where she'd died. There is a rock very close to the Ocean Pointe Resort on the edge of the coastline that the First Nations people considered sacred. That rock was considered sacred ground on which worship and rituals would take place. Since her death, the spirit of Agnes Bing has been seen wandering the rock for hours on end. She can also be seen walking up and down the shoreline near the hotel. People who walk along these spots often feel sad, cold, and lonely—even if there is no reason for them to feel that way at the moment.

POINT ELLICE BRIDGE

O N MAY 26, 1896, the city of Victoria was celebrating Queen Victoria's birthday. There were picnics, fairs, and, most exciting of all, a military exhibition at Macaulay Point in Esquimalt.

Getting from downtown Victoria to Macaulay Point meant hopping on the streetcar on Government Street, going a short way along Wharf Street, and then over the Point Ellice Bridge, which was built in 1885. Streetcars began going across the bridge in 1890, but the bridge was originally built for horse carts and pedestrians, not heavy streetcars. The city was aware of this. In 1892, they sent surveyors and repairman to drill holes in the bridge pilings to check the condition of the wood. They found that the wood was in bad shape and needed to be replaced, not just repaired. Four years later, nothing had been done to fix the pilings, and the holes that had been drilled in them had neither been filled nor repaired, hastening the rotting that had already begun. People continued to report that the bridge would sag whenever a streetcar went across, but those reports were ignored and the streetcars continued to cross the bridge.

At 1:40 PM on May 26, the city's inaction finally came with a price. Car number six, one of the older, smaller, and lighter streetcars, made its way safely across the bridge. As soon as it reached the other side, streetcar number sixteen, one of the larger, heavier new cars began its crossing. The car was built to carry a maximum of fifty-five people, but was actually carrying one hundred and forty people that day. The car had gone about a quarter of the way across when the bridge began to sway. The streetcar pressed on, and the swaying increased. With a terrifying crack, the bridge dropped about half a metre. The streetcar kept going. When it reached the centre of the Point Ellice Bridge, an even louder crack was heard throughout the harbour. The centre span of the bridge broke. Streetcar number sixteen plunged into the water, landing on its side. A few moments later, the main tracks and the rest of the span fell on top of the streetcar, trapping and killing even more people, including some who had managed to survive the first part of the disaster. Some lucky ones benefitted from the rest of the bridge collapsing, because it hit the streetcar with such force that it pushed them out through the broken windows. When it fell, the streetcar landed on some of the wood and ironwork that had broken off of the bridge when it first cracked. The car was actually pierced when it landed in the water, and then debris crushed even more of the car as the rest of the bridge collapsed on top of it.

Boats that had been cruising around the harbour saw what was going on and hurried to the disaster. Many people were saved because there were so many pleasure boats sailing around due to the birthday celebration. In all, fifty-five people died in the disaster and twenty-seven were seriously injured. The rescue effort soon became a recovery mission, with bodies being laid up on the beautiful lawns of nearby homes. People used tablecloths and curtains as shrouds for the victims. It was and still is the worst streetcar disaster in North American history.

The City of Victoria and the streetcar company were both found negligent: the streetcar company for overloading the car; the city for knowing the bridge was unsafe, making it more unsafe, and doing nothing about it. The compensation they were ordered to pay rendered the streetcar company bankrupt, and the city was almost broke for the next four years. The story was in the newspapers for months; there was not a single family in Victoria that had not been affected by the tragedy.

It seems that some people still aren't quite ready to give up looking for their loved ones lost in the disaster; they are not going to let a small consideration such as time have any bearing on whether or not they keep looking. In the 1890s, the banks of the Gorge were lined with big beautiful homes. Now, the only house left in that area is Point Ellice House. The rest of the properties lining the waterway have given way to industrial properties and warehouses. There is a path called the Galloping Goose Trail, which runs along an old rail line from downtown out to the other municipalities. Part of this trail goes under the new and improved Point Ellice Bridge, also known as the Bay Street Bridge. If you go down to the Galloping Goose Trail on a quiet night and stop just across from the old pilings from the Point Ellice Bridge, you may see proof of loved ones still searching. As you sit quietly, letting the atmosphere take you in, you will feel an eeriness surround you. If you look over to where the doomed bridge once spanned the water, you will notice something strange. Tiny lights, some yellow, some red, can be seen drifting over the surface of the water. They trail back and forth, only over one spot. Car lights do not reach that spot, nor do streetlights; it's simply an unexplained anomaly. After the bridge fell, many people were not recovered until the next day, but through the night there were boats full of searchers going back and forth over the sunken streetcar with lanterns attached to their small boats. Many who have witnessed these lights have said that you can even hear soft sighing noises that seem to go with the lights and their motion. Are these the sighs of the rescuers slowly giving up hope? Or the sighs of the dead who congregate around you, watching their searchers, knowing there is nothing left to look for?

ST. ANN'S ACADEMY
NATIONAL HISTORIC SITE

WHEN THE ROMAN Catholic nuns from the Quebec order of the Sisters of St. Ann answered a plea to come to the modest Fort Victoria in 1858 to teach the children of its approximately three hundred permanent residents, they had no idea what they were in for. Between the time they set sail and the time they arrived to run the little school, the Fraser River Gold Rush exploded. As a result, the sisters arrived to a town of thirty thousand, not three hundred. The sisters quickly overcame their shock and began holding classes in their log cabin convent. They had to expand their cabin before too long, and then ended up renting a bigger house in town. Finally, in 1860, the church began to build a proper convent on View Street. The View Street convent was eventually replaced with St. Ann's Academy, which was built in 1871. The nuns taught on this site, building on multiple additions over the years, until the academy closed in 1973. There is a small cemetery on the grounds, which was used from 1889 to 1908. After that, the sisters were interred at Ross Bay Cemetery. The building consists of four floors. The lower two floors housed the actual academy, the third floor housed the novitiate residences, and the fourth floor housed nuns exclusively. Thomas Hooper, the architect of many of Victoria's now-haunted buildings, including St. Joseph's hospital, designed St. Ann's Academy, which only further cements his reputation as Victoria's most haunted architect.

When the academy closed in the 1970s, the building faced an uncertain future. It was essentially mothballed, but still needed maintenance and care taking. A man named Tom was chosen for the job of night watchman. It wasn't long before he noticed things weren't quite right. Tom would hear all kinds of things in the supposedly empty building; he even gave nicknames to some of the entities. One night, his teenage son came with him to work. The boy had begged his dad to go with him because he wanted to see what the convent looked like inside. Tom reluctantly agreed. Once inside the old academy, Tom handed his son a flashlight and instructed him to stay in the building. He warned him not to go into the basement or up to the fourth floor. Tom had to go and do his route around St. Joseph's hospital, which he was also in charge of, then he would return to pick up his son.

As soon as his dad left, the teen headed directly for the fourth floor. As he began his ascent to the third floor, he noticed he was having trouble walking, almost as if he was being pushed backward. A black mist appeared in front of him. Even shining his flashlight at it did not diminish it. He determinedly kept climbing the stairs and finally made it up to the third floor, where he circled the staircase and started his ascent to the fourth floor. Remember, the fourth floor was for nuns only and a man certainly never would have been permitted on that floor. The determined teen had almost made it to the top of the stairs and onto the fourth floor, when suddenly he could no longer move. A white wall appeared before him and he physically could go no farther. Eventually, he gave up and headed for the basement. I would probably have skipped the basement and headed for the exit at this point, but not this guy.

As he went toward the basement and the kitchens, he heard voices, noises, and commotion. It sounded like a large party. The closer the boy got to the basement, the louder the noises became. He could hear the voices, but could not make out what they were saying. He heard pots clattering, food being chopped, and all the other sounds you would hear when a great meal is being prepared. The noise continued to grow as he got closer to the door. He reached for the door handle, but the moment his fingers touched the knob, the sound evaporated, like it had never been there. When he opened the door and went into the room, all he saw were his father's footsteps in the dust on the floor, going in the same circle his nightly route prescribed.

Over the years, others have reported feeling watched and seeing the former Mother Superior at the top of the grand staircase overlooking the hall below. On occasion, the chapel bell has rung when Ghostly Walks groups have been outside hearing the stories of the former academy and its spirit residents. It also happens quite late at the night when there is no one in the chapel. The bell only ever rings once.

Dawn Kirkham took a group into the academy to do an investigation there. She found some remarkable things and also had some physical things happen to her. The group was even able to assist one spirit to pass over.

While there are many spirits at the academy, three significant spirits, the ones who seem to be in charge, made themselves known to Dawn and her group. They found a grumpy priest who was a little bit nasty, but likely wouldn't do anyone harm, as well as a rather unpleasant and extremely territorial Mother Superior. They also discovered a young novice in the chapel, but she was hiding, scared of the other two. She seemed to be nice, but sad and timid. While the group was at the academy, a few of them got trapped in the confessional. The door simply would not open. It was not locked and there was no one else in the chapel, but they were stuck in there for a time. And when the group was in the organ room, the door handle jiggled up and down when no one was near it.

When the group was in the nuns' parlour, they all felt a significant vibe. There were six or eight people in the room, and they reached out to make contact with whoever was there. The MEL Metre (a device used to pick up on electromagnetic energy and also measure ambient temperature) went crazy; something was obviously attempting to communicate. They were able to connect with the entity—a young boy, six or seven years old, with severely disabled legs. The boy connected with one member of the group and this individual felt his sadness and loneliness very deeply. Thankfully, they were able to help the boy's spirit cross over and free him from remaining in the academy. It was a draining experience for the group, but they were all so grateful to have had the privilege of helping the boy move on.

While St. Ann's stood empty, its future unknown, Victorians grew anxious over rumours that it was going to be sold to a private developer. Early every morning, a security guard would clear the alcove of anyone who had decided to camp there overnight. One morning when he arrived he saw a group of nuns. They did not acknowledge him, but stared over toward the grave markers showing where the deceased nuns had been laid to rest. They never moved; they remained visible for quite some time, simply staring, until they faded away. They were seen a few more times until a statue of the Virgin Mary was installed among the graves like a protector. It seemed to do the trick and the group of nuns was not seen again.

In the gardens, altars have been placed where there used to be a playground for the students at the academy, now long since removed. Children's laughter has been heard in that area, so perhaps some of the students, even though they are long gone, return to play there with their school friends. Even today, custodians who work in the building after all of the officer workers have gone home have reported hearing the sound of large choirs of female voices, which seem to come from the empty chapel.

It would seem that although this building no longer serves its original purpose, it still holds true to those who built it and lived there.

HOME ON
FORT STREET

WHENEVER SOMEONE ASKS me to help with a spiritual predicament in their home, I never know what to expect. I always wonder if perhaps this will be it: this will be the time I don't experience anything and am unable to help. I worry that perhaps I've reached my full potential and maybe I wasn't very good at this type of thing in the first place. Most troubling can be the aspect of the unknown. I'm really not that brave, to be honest, and so the thought of running into something genuinely scary or evil is a bit daunting. However, whenever I go into these situations, I go with an open mind and an honest heart, and a desire to truly help someone live with something they may not understand.

In 2014, a friend of mine, Tani, moved into a new apartment. She had left her relationship, and while she was excited about her new life, she was also in need of a safe place to heal. The apartment she moved into was in the back of an old house on Fort Street. Tani and I had discussed spiritual matters before, so she knew that I have some ability or sensitivity to things that aren't seen. She had been experiencing some things that had left her a bit shaken—not scared necessarily, but certainly wanting to know more. She asked me if I would come by and check the place out. I walked over to her house on a warm summer evening, and as I approached the home I prepared myself to keep my spiritual ears open.

Tani had told me she had heard noises, things had moved, toilets had flushed, and lights had turned on and off. In addition, the spirit had showed some cognitive awareness because she had heard it call her name a few times. All of these signs are typical markers of a basic haunting.

I walked into the small, well-kept apartment, and immediately felt some kind of presence. I moved farther into the apartment and sat down in the living room. Tani poured tea and we began chatting. I had been wearing a cap that day, which is unusual for me, but seeing no reason to change before I went to Tani's, I kept it on. As we discussed the apartment, I suddenly got a very strong sense that I should take off my cap. I looked at Tani and said, "That's got to go." As I removed my cap, Tani looked at me with some surprise and said she didn't mind. I smiled and replied, "You don't, but he does."

The picture that had formed in my mind was of a man dressed in uniform. I wasn't sure from what era, but it was clear that he was a soldier and felt things should be done a certain way. One of those ways was that you did *not* wear a hat inside the house. In my head, I could see him standing in the kitchen with his arms behind his back and his hands clasped. I explained this to Tani, and she said, "So, you mean at ease?" It hadn't occurred to me, but it made perfect sense and was exactly what I meant. The soldier was standing at ease.

Some of the things that had been happening in her home she couldn't explain. She had heard her toilet flush in the middle of the night. I went and checked it out. It was a new toilet that was very difficult to flush by mistake. It was also on the other side of the apartment; there was no way the sound could have come from a toilet flushing in one of the other three apartments in the house.

One time, Tani said, while in the bath—a very deep, old-fashioned bath, which happened to be original to the home—she was about to fall asleep and slide down in the tub. Someone cleared their throat with an "Uh HUM" noise right beside her ear, which woke her up just before she slipped under the water.

Tani felt that whoever was there was benevolent and she did not feel threatened by it, but she was curious. One time she was woken in the middle of the night by a man's voice calling her name; it was soft, but distinct and persistent. At times she would be in bed reading when she would see movement out of the corner of her eye, but when she looked, there would be nothing there. One evening she turned off the light to go to sleep and distinctly heard the tap of a fork or spoon on a champagne flute right beside her ear. Other strange occurrences include an incident one evening when Tani was relaxing, reading a book on her couch. She had lit three candles in tall glass jars. The flames were shielded from the air; in fact, all of the windows were closed, and radiators heat the home. That didn't seem to stop one of the flames, and only one, from going crazy in the glass container while the other two remained still. Tani noticed it, put down her book, and said, "Stop that." The flame immediately stilled. After waiting for a few moments she said, "Okay, go ahead." The single flame began dancing yet again. On other occasions, her legs would go icy cold while the rest of her remained the same temperature. Tani had also heard her door close softly when no one else was in the room.

The impression I got from the soldier was that he approved of her. He liked her and trusted her and was glad she was in the house. I didn't want to upset Tani, but I also felt that perhaps he was protecting her from something else that might be in the house. I did mention that to her at the time, but with the very strong provision that I could be wrong and I didn't know for sure.

Once we felt that he had left us, we quickly got on the computer and typed in "military uniforms World War I and World War II." We got examples of both and soon realized that what I had seen would have been a uniform from the First World War. Tani wanted to know why he would still be in her house, why he had not moved on. I got the strong impression that he had died unexpectedly in the home. No one had anticipated his death, including him, but he liked being there. He felt comfortable, and he saw no reason to leave.

After a time, Tani became curious and wanted to know this soldier's name. For three nights, before she went to sleep, she would say out loud, "What's your name?" On the third night, she had just settled down and turned off the light, when she learned his name. Tani said when she closed her eyes that she saw nothing but green at first, and then words appeared on the green before fading away. She saw the words MY NAME IS appear individually, and then letters began to appear on the green, C, H, R, I. At this point, she said out loud, "Christopher?" With that, the next letter didn't appear but a single word did: "Yes."

I asked Tani to do some research on the house and to speak with the landlady to see if there was any link to what I had felt or sensed with some historical facts. I saw her again the following Monday and she was very excited. After talking to the landlady, she learned that the house had been a convalescent home for soldiers during the First and Second World Wars. The soldiers would have stayed there before ultimately being sent home. This fact was confirmed by an old newspaper article that Tani found while searching online for more information about the house. The landlady was very interested to hear what Tani had experienced as she too had experienced a presence in the house. Unlike Tani, the landlady spoke of a disapproving woman who was a frequent visitor and was most likely one of the original owners. This disapproving entity came to check on and, presumably, disapprove of the landlady quite often. While Tani had never sensed this disapproving woman, it now made sense to her why the soldier had communicated that he was there to help protect her.

At first everything was great for Tani in her apartment. But eventually things began to change. She came to me a few weeks after our initial meeting at her apartment. She mentioned that something odd had happened at her home and asked if I would be able to explain it. She said she'd been at home cleaning the living room and bedroom when she smelled something strange. She went into the kitchen and found that all of the burners on the stove had been turned to maximum, except the one that held a copper kettle. It was off. This stove was an older model, and everything about it was manual. I immediately thought that this might be some kind of warning, but of what? I asked Tani if she was doing anything different. She looked uncomfortable, but said no. I asked her if she thought it might be a warning of some kind. She didn't seem to think so. I was stumped. That was really the only thing that I had felt when she had told me about the burners. I thought it was a warning as the ghost had left the kettle alone. My interpretation was that turning on the burners wasn't about harming Tani— it was simply designed to get her attention. I suggested she perhaps ask the soldier if there was something upsetting him.

A few weeks later she told me that she had met a new guy and he was actually staying with her on a pretty frequent basis. I looked at her and asked he if stayed for the first time before or after the stove burners turned on? She looked sheepish and replied that the incident occurred the morning after her new friend had stayed over for the first time. I think we figured out what the warning was about. The new man in her life eventually moved in and Tani received one more message from the ghost. This time the only burner that was turned to maximum was the burner holding the copper kettle. All of the other burners were off. Thankfully the kettle still had water in it so it hadn't boiled dry, but it was close. This seemed to be the ghost sending another message. Was he jealous? Did he not approve of her new guy? Did he not approve of having "gentleman callers" stay over? Perhaps it was the disapproving woman's spirit who felt so strongly about the matter that she was able to push past Christopher and make her point. Either way, while Christopher still made his presence known to Tani from time to time, and she still found his company soothing, he never did anything when her new friend, now husband, was around.

Tani has since moved out of the apartment, but not for the reason you might think. She lived there quite peacefully, even with the presence of spirits. But after she met her new love, they bought a house together. While I know that she didn't mind having the spirit in her apartment, she hopes her new home will only house the living. Time will tell...

THE YOUNG BUILDING—
CAMOSUN COLLEGE

THE YOUNG BUILDING, which is part of the Lansdowne Campus of Camosun College, has, like many other buildings in Victoria, had a varied life. It opened in 1914 as the Victoria Normal School (an old-fashioned term for a teachers' college), the first of its kind in town. In the 1940s, it was turned into a military hospital, complete with an operating theatre and a morgue. After the war was over, it reverted back to being a school and included a new institution called Victoria College, which shared the building. In 1971, it became the first building of the newly created Camosun College.

There have long been multiple stories about the Young Building that involve strange goings-on. Students, instructors, and even security staff and custodians—the standard and most reliable sources of ghost stories for large public buildings—have reported these happenings.

When I first moved to Victoria, I took a few evening classes in the Young Building. I hadn't heard anything about the building, but I know what I felt. My classes were on the third floor and while I didn't enjoy climbing those stairs at six PM, I dreaded going down them even more at nine PM. Going up the stairs felt like moving through a mist or fog, but it felt even more threatening a few hours later when I had to leave. I actually forgot about those sensations over the years, but when I returned to the Young Building recently as part of my research for this book, I experienced the same feelings again all these years later. I expected that the bottom floor would be the most active, and indeed there is activity there, but for the most part, the third floor holds the most active energy and the most troublesome or helpful (depending on their moods, I suppose) spirits.

Our first story comes from security guard Christine Crawley. Christine worked at the Young Building for fifteen years. She is not a woman prone to flights of fancy; her matter-of-fact demeanour backs that up. While Christine was happy to share her experiences, she was certainly quick to point out that while strange things happen, most can be explained. Some, however, cannot. There was more than one time when Christine felt uncomfortable at the college, and there are certain areas where she didn't linger, places where she would do her required check-ins and exit quickly. One time while guarding the building, she heard voices and thumping in the elevator. Thinking quickly, she called the elevator down to where she was and stepped back, expecting to deal with at least a couple of people who had no business being in the building. As the elevator came closer, the voices and thumping grew louder. Christine prepared herself. Right up until the moment the elevator doors opened, the noises continued to get louder. The second the doors parted, the elevator fell silent—it was empty. Christine could not explain that.

One experience in particular forced Christine to be a little more open minded about paranormal activities. It happened when she was training a new security guard. The young woman was very interested in seeing the roof and the clock tower on the Young Building. Christine wasn't thrilled about going up there as she knew it was under construction and the handrails had been taken down, but the young guard was so excited about seeing it that Christine agreed to take her up, giving her many warnings and reminders to be extra careful and cautious as they ascended the ladder to the tower.

Christine went first and climbed onto the roof. As she took her first step, she felt her foot slip and she began to fall forward, right off the roof. Just as she was about to tumble off, she felt a hand grab her jacket and pull her back from falling head first down the roof. As she stood panting, she turned to thank the young guard, assuming it was her who had steadied her. When she looked back, she realized that the other woman was still on the ladder and hadn't actually made it out of the roof hatch yet. Severely spooked, Christine told the young woman they were going right back down, but as she descended the ladder, Christine turned back and said to the air over the roof, "Thanks, Casper," before she closed the hatch behind her. At the best of times, Christine had an uncomfortable relationship with the unseen residents of the Young Building, but she had to admit that at least once, they definitely did more good than harm.

Lisa, an instructor who has been at the college for over fifteen years, told me one of the most unique stories I've ever heard. It was early in the morning and she was just coming into her office. Nothing seemed amiss or creepy. It was a regular winter morning, so it was still dark outside at that hour. As she walked down the hall, she saw her friend, who also worked in the building, in the reflection of the glass doors at the end of the hall. He was creeping comically up behind her, with his arms up and lifting his legs melodramatically, like a vampire in a silent movie. Lisa laughed and stopped. She put her hands on her hips and said, "I can totally see you!" As she stood there waiting for him to catch up, she didn't turn around. She kept watching his reflection. He was just about to reach her, when, as Lisa described, "It was like he was a water-colour painting and someone had just poured a glass of water on him. He just melted right in front of me." Of course, when this happened, she spun around to see, but no one was there. She spun back around to look at the reflection, but nothing was there either. Nothing like that has ever happened again, but it troubled her. How did whatever was in the hall with her mimic her friend? Was it being funny to make her laugh, or was it a deliberate attempt to fool her into lowering her guard?

Ed Sum was a student at the college in 2008. Ed had always been interested in ghosts and the paranormal. Soon after starting at Camosun, he began hearing stories about the Young Building. While Ed believes in ghosts, he focuses on proof of their exis-tence, not feelings or hunches. He wants to see and hear things, and even more importantly, he wants to record the experience. He was working as a reporter for the Camosun newspaper at the time and got permission to investigate the tales he'd heard about the building with a paranormal group he was part of. Some said that the third floor was very unsettled, particularly the bath-rooms, but other parts of the building were unsettled too. In the old auditorium, the piano could be heard playing on its own. The changing room on the bottom floor was originally used as a morgue, and several people had mentioned feeling uncomfortable down there.

When Ed brought in the paranormal investigators, they expe-rienced a number of interesting occurrences. One of the most irrefutable pieces of evidence they gathered was a recording. Investigative groups use voice recorders in an attempt to catch electronic voice phenomena, or EVPs. These occur because spirit voices seem to be able to be caught on voice recorders rather than by human ears. One of the investigators asked the room, "What time is it?" When they played the tape back later to review for possible evidence, the answer was there. But it wasn't a voice that belonged to any of the investigators. "Eleven," it said. The time was exactly eleven PM.

This EVP was definitely not a one-off. When the Camosun College radio station was on air, they often had difficulty recording announcements and commercials. The recordings would be repeatedly polluted with voices, whispering, and chatter. These background voices were definitely audible, but no one could tell what they said. The same problem happened when people attempted to do voice-overs for student video projects; repeated takes had to be made as mysterious voices kept showing up on the recordings.

It wasn't just voices that made themselves known. The photography students talked about one of the darkrooms and the way it was set up, with stations where each student could do their work. There was always one station where the focusing magnifier would go missing. The poor student would then go in search of it. When the student finally gave up the search and returned to their station, the missing piece of equipment would always be there, waiting for them.

Linda, an instructor at Camosun, told me one of the most chilling stories I've heard about the Young Building. Linda had taught at the college for more than ten years and had spent a lot of time in the Young Building. A self-professed skeptic, Linda wasn't in a hurry to talk about her experience, but she was also aware that it was undeniable and she had no explanation for what happened.

Linda was working late one night and needed to print a document. Unfortunately for her, the printer on her floor was not working. She had to send the print job up to a printer on the third floor, which was situated in an alcove that led to four locked office doors. It was around nine PM and dark inside and out. If you have ever been in the Young Building, you know it's quite a dark building at the best of times, but it was certainly darker that night as Linda climbed the stairs to the third floor. She walked through the doors to the third floor, turned left, and made her way to the printer.

It was quiet up there. Linda knew she was the only one on that floor, if not in the whole building. When she got to the alcove, she noticed her document wasn't completely done printing. She stood waiting, facing the printer with her back to the hallway. At that moment, she felt someone breathing on the back of her neck. At the time she had long hair, so someone would have to have been quite close for her to feel their breath on her neck. Linda turned on her heel to find she was still completely alone. As it was cold outside, no windows were open and the hallways were heated only with radiators; there was no other source of airflow. Linda gathered her papers and went straight back to her office, where she collected her things and left for the night—distinctly unsettled and less skeptical than she had been before.

And then there was Alan, who was twenty-three when he took a job as security guard at Camosun—a job he kept for only one year. On the night he quit that job, he responded to a "triggered alarm" at the Young Building—something had set off the motion sensors. This happened quite often as the Young Building had a very high incidence of triggered alarms. Alan hated this part of the job. Just after three AM, he went to the school and started his rounds on the third floor, making his way down to the basement without finding anyone else in the building. As he began to walk along the hallway of the basement area, he suddenly knew he wasn't alone; he felt a very strong presence. "I'm not here to harm you. I just need to check the building," he called out. At that moment, the basement lights began to turn off, one by one, starting at the far wall and coming toward him. It was a defining moment. Alan turned, walked out of the building, and vowed to never come back.

There is also the story that a long-time custodian, Norm, told me. He was on the third floor one evening in the middle of the night, attempting to complete the long and arduous task of buffing the floors in the main hallway. As he went about his task, he didn't notice anything usual. Norm was used to the eccentricities of the building, and wasn't phased by much. That is, until all of the doors lining the hallway closed at the same time. He took that as a sign, and went to go find something else to do on another floor for the evening.

Before I began collecting these stories, I wandered the building to see what I might sense. I expected the basement, where the morgue had been, to be the most unsettled, but it wasn't. The third floor has the basement beat.

From what I could tell, the spirits in the building, of which there are certainly more than a couple, are generally happy. They enjoy the vibe that is there during the day, and don't mind having some young, fresh energy around them. As it is most likely that these are leftover spirits from the time when the building was a military hospital, this isn't that surprising. Young soldiers make young ghosts. However, nighttime is when the college is truly their domain. While they will put up with people being around—custodians, instructors, security guards, and the like—there is a much higher chance the spirits will make themselves known after dark. A great example of this is the number of false hits this building gets on its security system; guards are continually summoned to find nothing amiss, but with an alarm to reset, nonetheless. The spirits that have remained in the Young Building are not looking for trouble, or even, from what I could tell, to move on to the next realm. They are simply carrying on with what they've always done. If I had to guess, I would say they'll keep doing so for a while longer.

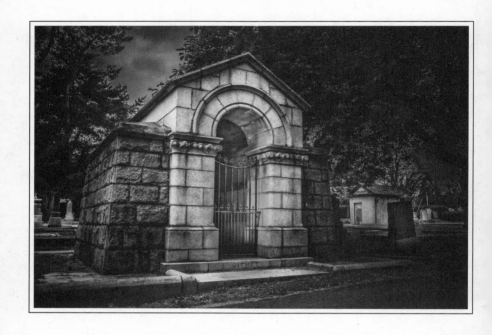

ROSS BAY CEMETERY

THE ROSS BAY Cemetery, the third graveyard to be built in the Victoria area, opened in 1873. It is on 27.5 acres adjacent to the ocean and was named after Isabella Ross, who donated the land for the cemetery. Isabella was a Métis woman, and the first independent female landowner in British Columbia. Isabella's son was buried there in 1876. Her grave is across the path from his; she was buried in 1885.

Graveyards are not generally full of spirits because most spirits choose to remain with their families or at the homes they lived in when they were alive. Ross Bay seems to be an exception. I have certainly felt energy when I have gone there. Once I started doing some research, I found I wasn't the only one.

One man, a former groundskeeper at the cemetery, had a long and involved conversation with another man, who said he was a former groundskeeper at the cemetery himself. They discussed technical aspects of grounds keeping. The former employee seemed quite knowledgeable and even gave the current groundskeeper some excellent tips on maintenance that hadn't occurred to him. It wasn't until a few days later when the groundskeeper mentioned his conversation to a colleague that he learned that the man had died on the job several years earlier.

A lady in black has been seen in the cemetery, lingering over a child's grave. People see her walking around, but when they look back, she's gone. The cemetery is flat, and the only thing obstructing views are the trees, but they are not big enough to allow a person to disappear. The lady in black is not the only person to have been seen wandering around before vanishing; this is a fairly common occurrence at the Ross Bay Cemetery.

Troy Reid—the same Troy Reid who saw a First Nations construction worker's spirit at the Empress—had an experience in the graveyard he won't soon forget. One night he was walking through the cemetery when he came to a mausoleum that wasn't actually there. The graveyard is officially closed at night to deter vandalism, so perhaps the spirits become more protective after dark. Troy certainly felt this. At the same time he was seeing the phantom mausoleum, he was also overcome by a female spirit that stopped him in his tracks; it was so powerful he couldn't breathe. Troy was eventually able to tear himself away, and got out of the cemetery as fast as he could.

Ross Bay Cemetery became the final home for many of British Columbia's most elite and influential citizens. There are a number of mausoleums in the graveyard that reflect the wealth and stature of those within. The Dunsmuir mausoleum has a substantial energy, as does the McKenzie mausoleum.

The energy near the Dunsmuir mausoleum is significant and understandable. Robert Dunsmuir was one of the wealthiest men in British Columbia because he struck it rich in the coal industry. Robert and his family were *the* power people of British Columbia for many years, and they were used to having people do what they asked. They also left their mark on the city: Robert left behind Craigdarroch Castle, and his son built Hatley Castle. People looking to do ghost investigations at the mausoleum have found that their cameras will malfunction when they attempt to take pictures there. Blank screens and shadowed pictures are all that come out, but once you move away from the mausoleum, everything returns to normal. The Dunsmuirs were a pretty stubborn bunch, so I'm not surprised they seem to still be trying to control things from beyond the grave.

The McKenzie family established their final resting place so the whole family could be together, but one son, who chose to gamble and drink his life away, was disinherited and, when he died, was refused entry into the family crypt. It seems he hasn't stopped trying to get in. On stormy nights, people would see a shadowy figure slip into the mausoleum itself. This sight became so well known that the family, fearing someone was living in the mausoleum, had an iron gate installed on the crypt to keep anyone out. However the darkened figure is still seen seeking shelter inside the mausoleum today.

Dawn Kirkham had a rather startling experience at the cemetery. While never having gone to the cemetery to do an investigation, she was there one afternoon helping out on a cemetery tour, which was a fundraiser for the upkeep and restoration of the cemetery. She says she was accosted by two spirits. One was the spirit of the son of a famous Victoria spiritualist named James, who had died in the war. Though he was killed in Europe, his spirit returned to the only grave marker he ever knew: the one in Ross Bay Cemetery.

The other spirit was a bit more disturbing. It was an older woman who was clearly insane. This woman was wearing a dirty white nightgown; she had long nails, filthy hands and feet, and wild grey hair. The woman kept yelling in Dawn's face. She alternated between high-pitched laughing and sobbing. It's interesting to note that at this point in the tour, the group was very close to where Isabella Ross's house had been. After her death, her house had been used as an insane asylum. The woman, thankfully, did not follow Dawn around, but stayed where she was so Dawn was able to move away from her.

Andrew Merpaw, a local ghost hunter, also had some interesting things happen to him in the cemetery. One time he was attempting to do a paranormal investigation, when he saw some glowing orbs in a monkey puzzle tree. He also started to hear church bells. While this was puzzling enough, crows then began to circle overhead. Andrew looked around, and realized that he was standing next to the grave of David Fee, a man who was murdered on Christmas Eve when he was leaving the cathedral after mass. David has also been reported as showing up as a white mist to startled walkers and visitors to the cemetery.

Other things to look for in the cemetery include the ghost of Isabella Ross, looking out to sea with a sad, downcast look on her face. Something else seems to linger near the largest angel in the graveyard. An older couple, dressed in full Victorian finery, are said to glide through the western part of the graveyard from time to time.

No matter where you go in this graveyard, there is a chance you will encounter something, be it fascinating and peaceful, or disturbing and anxiety inducing.

OUTSIDE
OF TOWN

HOTEL ON
LOCHSIDE DRIVE

WHAT HAPPENS IF a family loses a child and his spirit remains, but the family leaves? Loneliness. Overwhelming loneliness and a really terrible night's sleep.

This is not the first hotel I've stayed in that was haunted, but it is probably one of the saddest.

In 2009, my former wife, Margaret, received a two-night stay at a local hotel chain's first attempt at running a boutique-style hotel. The hotel was in a large, gracious home on Lochside Drive, which had been built in the mid-1980s. As our son was quite young at the time, Margaret decided she'd take the first night alone, and I would join her for the second. An uninterrupted bath and a solid night's sleep were too strong an allure to be ignored.

Margaret will tell you that she doesn't have much time for ghosts—and the poor woman was married to me. However, I dispute this to some extent based on my observations of her. Margaret is actually very sensitive to what's going on around her, even if she doesn't link it to the paranormal. I respect this; we all have boundaries, and with a smile and a nod she would patiently listen to me tell her the latest ghost story that I'd come across. She was with me for more than one experience of the ghostly kind, so she knows it's not all made up, but she is not keen to talk about it.

I spoke with Margaret the morning after her first night in the hotel. When I asked how she had enjoyed her night of peaceful slumber, she responded that she hadn't. She couldn't put her finger on why she had such a restless night. "Was it noisy? Did other guests keep you awake?" I asked. Margaret said no. In fact, she was currently the only guest staying at the hotel and the manager/hostess slept in a different building. This restless night's sleep was unusual for her, but we wrote it off as the result of being in a strange room. We even joked that by now she was probably used to never sleeping through the night, and this was probably why she hadn't.

I arrived at the hotel later that afternoon. I was looking forward to this mini-getaway and also to staying in a luxurious boutique hotel. I drove through the gates and down the long, beautifully landscaped paved driveway. The first thing I noticed was a guest cottage close to the driveway. (The house itself was farther back.) It was a single-storey building, long and low, that almost hugged the ridge on which it was built. The main house, now hotel, was a combination of pale stone and beige woodwork with a lot of rectangular windows. Past the house was a large well-manicured garden that sloped gently and invitingly to the ocean and a rocky beach.

As I pulled up, Margaret and the manager came out to greet me. At first I thought, *How fancy*, then I realized we were literally the only three people there. Margaret was relieved to see me, and the young manager, Julia, was bright and energetic. She welcomed me in, asked if we wanted anything to drink, and then left us on our own. The interior of the house was unique. There was a large hall just in through the main door, branching left and right. On the right was the largest single room I'd ever seen in a house. It combined a kitchen, a sunken living room, and a dining room. The wall facing the ocean was entirely made of glass, and the view was spectacular. There were a few other rooms down the right-hand hallway, but they were bathrooms and storage rooms. Down the left hall were several doors angled away from the hall, which were the bedrooms. Margaret took me down to our room so I could dump my bag. Already I was feeling something quite strong.

The farther we went down the hall, the more pronounced the feeling became. As soon as I had entered the house, my Spidey senses had gone off, but I couldn't yet identify why. As we moved down the hall, it was like getting closer to a light bulb; the sensation intensified. When we got into the bedroom, I dropped my bag and said, "I'm really sorry, but I have got to see what else is in here."

"Oh," my wife said casually, "there's a swimming pool at the end of the hall, but that's it." I was impressed there was an indoor pool, but at the same time, a little voice was triumphantly saying, "Aha!" I knew that whatever it was—or I should say whoever it was—was going to be in the pool area. I asked Margaret if she had already been in the pool, which she had. Margaret is an excellent swimmer and really loves the water, but she admitted that she hadn't stayed very long in the pool. She wasn't sure why, but the pool made her uncomfortable. *Huh*, I thought, *sounds like my kind of pool!*

As much as I wanted to get to the pool straightaway, as I exited the room and turned right, the feeling became even more pronounced and seemed to project down the hall. Odd. I began almost inching my way down the hall, stopping outside each of the other bedroom doors as I passed them. When I was within three doors of the pool entrance, I became overwhelmed by emotion. It seemed to be blasting out of the pool area and was incredibly powerful. It was a feeling of sadness, misery, and confusion. I was freaked out. I had never encountered anything like this before. Its sheer power and presence was terrifying, yet there was nothing scary about what was coming out of the pool area.

I made my way slowly to the door to the pool and pulled it open. I walked halfway around the pool and almost felt like crying. There was a boy, around seven or eight years old, in the pool area. In fact, he never left. This child spent most of his time crying and pleading. I got some pictures and knew he had drowned, but I couldn't figure out why he was still here and so upset. As a guest, wouldn't he have moved on? I had certainly not heard anything about a child drowning at the hotel, and I was pretty sure that would have made the local news. I tried to communicate love and peace and comfort to him, but he was oblivious and just so sad. I didn't even make it all the way around the pool before I turned and headed back to the room.

Once in the room, I gave Margaret my usual detailed report with enough scope for her to really appreciate it. "There's definitely something there," I said. "Yeah, I figured," she responded glumly. We spoke no more of it.

That night we headed out for dinner with the joy that only new parents set free can feel. As we drove back to the hotel, we were both looking forward to a good night's sleep in a fancy bed. As I turned up the darkened driveway, the sense of sadness began to settle over us. Somehow I did not believe a solid rest was going to be had in this place, no matter how beautiful and luxurious it was.

Unfortunately, I was proven correct. Throughout the night, I was woken many times. The emotions were very strong and there was no reprieve. Margaret was woken many times, too.

When morning finally came, we got up, showered, and headed to the kitchen, where breakfast was to be served as part of our room package. There were two other couples in the hotel now. One sat in the dining room, the other out on the deck. Margaret and I sat at the breakfast bar overlooking the stove where Julia was cooking breakfast.

Here came the tricky part: How could I bring up the fact that something had happened in the pool area without freaking her out, or even worse, having her clam up? Once a hotel is old and established, many enjoy a resident ghost. But if a hotel is just starting up, it does not need that kind of stigma. I proceeded slowly, asking if she was the only staff here. There was a gardening team that came once a week, but otherwise Julia was the only staff, responsible for the front desk, cooking, cleaning, bartending, and hosting. I asked a bit about the house. Julia was very forthcoming, explaining it was one of three grand houses the owners of the local chain had bought to try out the concept of boutique accommodation.

Julia exclaimed that she loved her job, and was excited to be a part of the hotel venture. I asked how the house had come to be bought by the hotel chain. She told me a German industrialist and his family had owned it as a summer home. The family decided they no longer wanted the home, so they packed up and headed back to Germany and sold the house to the hotel chain. I cautiously continued with another question, asking if anything unfortunate had ever occurred in the house. Julia looked guarded and asked what I meant. I said, "Well, for example, in the pool area. Anything with kids?" Julia looked uncomfortable. She admitted that one of the family's three boys had drowned in the pool. The parents were devastated and sold the place as quickly as possible to get away from the memory of their son's tragic death. I exhaled. I hadn't noticed I was holding my breath. I told Julia, "I think he's still there." She got a bit of a twinkle in her eye, leaned over, and said, "Why do you think I live in the guesthouse?"

After breakfast, we didn't really feel like sticking around. I left Margaret to finish her packing and headed toward the pool one last time. No one else was in there. I said out loud to the boy, "It's okay. You can go." I told him he didn't need to be trapped here, and that while I didn't know who, I could guarantee that someone was waiting for him and he'd be so much happier there.

Did he go? I felt the room sigh, and the emotions lessen, but I don't really know if he left. This was the first time I'd ever encountered a spirit who was so unhappy where they were residing that I was compelled to do something. While I don't usually mess with the ghosts and their situations, this was definitely a different case.

I don't know if it was the haunted pool, lack of interest, or poor management, but within months the house gates were closed, a FOR SALE sign went up, and the hotel was closed for good. The gates remained closed for several months before the house was bought as a private home. For a long time, the new owners had a sign up in front of their house that read: THIS IS NO LONGER A HOTEL. THIS IS A PRIVATE HOME. PLEASE DO NOT DRIVE DOWN THE DRIVEWAY. I did venture down the drive, just once, after the sale. The home no longer had the same sad aura that had been so powerful months before, but I don't know if the boy left, or just became quieter.

THE WILKINSON JAIL

THE COMPLEX OF buildings now known as the Vancouver Island Regional Correctional Centre, the Wilkinson Jail, or "the Wilkie" has had a rich and storied life, which may explain why so many spirits and ghosts still wander the halls. In researching this building, I not only had the opportunity to talk to a couple of correctional officers, I also had a chance to tour the facility and get my own impressions of this rather foreboding institution.

It started as the Saanich Prison Farm. It was built in 1914 to welcome thirty-eight prisoners from the old jail, which itself had been built to replace the original jail in Bastion Square in downtown Victoria. The second jail had been partially destroyed by fire in 1912. Rather than rebuild it, the government decided to build a new twenty-five-acre prison farm.

The prison was built for the princely sum of 100,000 dollars, 2.4 million dollars today. It was designed by William Ridgway Wilson, the same gentleman who designed the Bay Street Armoury. It was built to house up to 140 prisoners, with room to bring in forty additional beds. There were also outbuildings and barns built by the prisoners, but these were removed in 1985 when the prison was modernized. Surprisingly, the Saanich Prison Farm was only in operation for three years. It closed in 1917 to save money—and to send prisoners to fight in the First World War.

The Colquitz Mental Home was located in the building from 1919 to 1964. The hospital was home to a wide range of criminally and dangerously insane men. These men worked the farm grounds that were then still part of the facility; as it turns out, they were great farmers. In the 1930s, the patients produced 90,000 pounds of vegetables, 4,000 pounds of fruit, and 15,000 pounds of meat. It wasn't all fun and games though. During the 1920s, there were numerous escapes. While the site was being used as a mental hospital and farm, several additional buildings were constructed on the property, along with other attractions such as fishponds, greenhouses, barns, stables, and even a tennis court. These were all built by the patients.

During this time, there were also several deaths as many of the patients weren't so much insane as they were hard to care for. Institutionalizing people was done as a matter of course in those days. These patients were often not in great health to begin with, but you have to wonder if being locked up with people who were certifiably or criminally insane shortened their lifespans further.

After almost forty-five years as a mental home, the building reverted to its original purpose and became the Oakalla Prison Farm in 1966. Within a few years it was renamed the Vancouver Island Regional Correctional Centre, which is still its official name, but it is commonly known as the Wilkie.

Regardless of its name or its use, the building has seen its share of trouble. Violence, escapes, and even the murder of a police officer in the 1960s have all occurred on the grounds. The combination of jail and mental hospital is a good recipe for unrest and ghosts.

One of the correctional officers had an experience a few years ago. He was sitting in one of the units, which have kitchens and seating areas with cells off to the side. He was right in the middle of the castle façade. The windows in the façade were all closed. The officer was doing some paperwork when he heard what he thought was the wind picking up, but he didn't think much of it. After that he heard a clunk, looked up, and saw the coffee pot fly off the counter. It travelled nine or ten feet, and then hit the wall. It hit the wall with such force that the handle broke and the metal pot was dented from the impact. Needless to say, the officer didn't spend a whole lot of time up there alone anymore.

Another officer spoke of something that happened in another original site unit. He was there alone when he heard a deep rhythmic thumping noise coming from a wing that was under renovation and therefore empty. It started out quite faint, but became more noticeable. As he lingered alone in the unit doing his checks, the noise got louder and louder. He finished his checks, which he did thoroughly, but admittedly in a hurry, and got out of there as quick as he could. So far he has not needed to go back.

There are many other stories of noises, particularly the sound of doors closing, which is odd as all the doors are locked as standard procedure. People often hear voices, footsteps, and other inexplicable sounds.

These stories are not limited to the officers either. A former guest of the jail shared a story about being in his cell. One night he was woken by what he thought was his cellmate trying to get in his upper bunk with him. He could feel something cold and solid all the way up his back and felt the blankets being tugged. The inmate jumped off the bunk only to see his cellmate in his own bed, wrapped in his blanket, facing the wall, and sleeping deeply. The poor man was so affected by this experience that he begged the correctional officer to put him in another cell. The officer agreed to; he admitted that he too had experienced strange things, and so had many other officers and inmates. That particular cell was known for being the source of strange laughter, even when it was completely empty. It was always the same slightly mocking laugh, though the inmates changed on a regular basis as this particular section of the jail was for stays no longer than thirty days.

When I was in the prison, I was struck by quite a number of different presences that remain within the walls. The impression I got was that they were not from the time when the facility was a prison, but more likely from its time as a mental hospital. The ones who have remained are quite likely not even aware they are dead, and are also likely to cause trouble. I didn't get the impression that they are malicious, but they are certainly active and enjoy scaring people; officers or inmates—it doesn't matter to them—although they're likely to go a little easier on the inmates as they will see them as compatriots.

Go past the Wilkie on your next drive around Victoria. What do you feel? Anything of note? This really is a fascinating site and one we are lucky to have been able to keep around for so long.

HOME ON ELK
LAKE DRIVE

As far as ghost tales usually go, this home is certainly a unique setting. On a warm summer night in 2014, my friend Corrina, who is also sensitive to spirits, and I headed to a large, well-kept modern townhouse. The townhouse had been built in 1994, so it hardly qualified for your typical old-building ghost quotient. Nonetheless, a mutual friend, aware of our sensitivities, had invited us to her home to see if we could figure out what was going on.

Our friend Sheila, the home's owner, is a strong woman, with a positive outlook and a tonne of energy. As a single mom with a demanding full-time job, Sheila did not have any time left over for whatever was going on in her home. While Shelia is a self-professed non-believer, it was hard to dismiss that strange things were happening, with annoying constancy. The light bulbs kept burning out. It is of course normal to have a bulb burn out now and then, but three or four a week was excessive. Items fell off the shelves. No breeze or vibrations preceded these objects falling, but it was more or less a daily occurrence. Sheila was uncertain, but she wasn't afraid.

Corrina and I pulled into the courtyard of the townhouse complex and got out of the car. I was immediately hit with a sense of awe and power regarding a tree in the middle of the courtyard. It was obviously very old, and I was drawn to it in the strangest way.

I definitely felt a presence out there and was looking forward to going into the home and seeing what was what.

Upon entering the home, my "antennae" were up full blast. We sat down to have tea in the kitchen and talk about what was going on. Sheila was puzzled by the instances, and thought it might be nice to see if Corrina and I could pick anything up. We began to tour the house. It was a large home. There was a fully finished basement with a rec room, bedroom, and bathroom. The main floor consisted of a large kitchen, living room, and dining room. The upstairs had three bedrooms and two bathrooms. The trouble was, I felt nothing. Not a hint, not a whisper, nothing. This was a bit embarrassing. I had shown up to help and I honestly couldn't sense even a touch of a presence.

As we returned to the main floor, I looked at Corrina and asked, "Anything?"

"No," she replied, "nothing. You?"

"Not even a little. This is so weird," I responded. We were about halfway down the stairs when I noticed the sliding glass doors to the back patio. I was suddenly struck by the feeling that I had to be out there. It was really important. I looked at Sheila and asked, "May I go out there?" She nodded yes and I was out the door.

I looked to my left and my right; there was a long line of identical decks, one at the back of each unit. Then there was about twenty feet of grass. There was quite a heavy band of trees at the end of the grass; it was thick enough that I couldn't see through the trees. By this point, Sheila and Corrina had joined me on the deck and were leaning on the railing like I was. I was a bit mystified as to what I was doing out there when I suddenly got a whole lot of pictures in my head and knew what was going on.

I pointed to the trees. "Is there a stream or creek in those trees?" I asked. Sheila confirmed there was. I then pointed to the left, almost to the end of the row of townhouses, "And is there a farmhouse down there in the trees?" At this she looked a bit startled, but responded that yes, there was indeed the foundation of an old farmhouse deep within the trees.

I was so relieved because I'd figured it out—or had been told what was going on and it suddenly all made sense. The farmer whose land we were now on was still very much there, but instead of haunting the houses, he remains on his land. I explained that the water was a forceful attractant; it is a power source. Combine the power of water with the fact that the farmer had no desire to leave and that sort of sealed the deal.

The good thing for Sheila was this farmer had no intention of or interest in haunting her home. What he did want was for her to know that this was his land, and as far as he was concerned, she was his tenant. I also said, with some weird confidence, that now that she knew his feelings, and he knew she was aware of them, she wasn't going to be bothered anymore.

I took a guess and asked her if the other residents had experienced the same kind of electrical problems she had. At this point, she got a funny look on her face and confided that the strata had in fact hired an electrician to examine all of the wiring in the complex because of "problems," but he had found nothing wrong. I laughed because it's always nice to have some kind of confirmation and there it was. The farmer also thought it was pretty funny that they had brought in an electrician. He wasn't a mean guy, but he was in charge and was used to having things go his way. My impression was that he had grown old and died on the land he loved and that, as he was one of the first people to farm this land, he couldn't bear to leave it. I'm not sure he was aware that he was dead, but he was certainly aware that others were on his land—not that he minded, but he wanted to be clear with them that they were on his property.

I met up with Sheila about three months later. We were in a work environment so I didn't want to say anything too open and out there. But I gave her a meaningful look and said, "So?"

She looked back at me with a big smile and responded happily, "Nothing." It appears the farmer was pleased. Everyone knew who was boss and now he could get back to focusing on what he really cared about: his land and the large tree that had so caught my attention when we'd driven in. It was the only thing on his land that hadn't changed, and he was very drawn to it and loved it. As far as I know, the farmer is still there, and new owners of the townhouse units should move in prepared with a warehouse pack of light bulbs.

VICTORIA-AREA
LAKE HOUSE

RIENDS OF MINE were going away for the summer, so they
offered up their beautiful Victoria–area lake house to any of
their friends who wanted to book a week or a weekend.
The only rule was you had to leave it nice for the people coming
after you.

Our family thought this was a great deal. We reserved our
week, and even invited our friend Stephanie, who was coming
from the Maritimes for a visit, to stay there with us. We congratulated ourselves on our luck and were looking forward to a fun
escape and enjoying the cottage lifestyle.

I won't go into a lot of detail about where the cottage is, as the
generous people who lent it out still live there. As cool as they
are, they're not really anxious to have their home turned into
a drive-by spectacle. I don't blame them. I will say that it is an
older house, built in the 1960s or 1970s. It is a single-storey home
with dark wood siding. The front door is in the centre with two
wings angled out on either side. The interior is lined with pine
that has mellowed into a rich, dark golden colour. However, as a
result of all that wood, the house seemed very dark, right from the
moment we stepped in the door.

My wife and I took a room on the side of the house where there
were three bedrooms and a bathroom; Stephanie took a room in

the other wing of the house, which had two bedrooms, a bathroom, and a dining room. We took some time to unpack and settle in, then met in the middle, where the kitchen, living room, and generous deck were. Even before we had begun to make our first meal, Stephanie and I both heard creaks and clunks from the house. Something wasn't sitting right, but we both agreed we didn't know the house that well, and so we recognized it could be the sounds of an older, all-wood house settling down as the day cooled. We had our dinner, watched the sunset, and retired for the night.

The next morning when I got up to make coffee I was quite surprised to find Stephanie fast asleep on the couch. I moved around as quietly as I could, but coffee first thing in the morning is not something that can be delayed. Unfortunately, I made enough noise to wake her up. I asked why she was sleeping on the couch, and she replied that she had had a very rough night and needed to get out of her room because she just couldn't stay asleep in there. I looked at her quizzically. Stephanie had known me for a long time. We had spoken of our own experiences with ghosts and were not afraid to talk about the paranormal together.

We got on with our day, doing all the usual things you do at a lakeside cottage: hanging out on the dock, floating around in tubes, going for walks, and just enjoying the outdoors. We eventually got hungry enough to go in for dinner. It was starting to cool down a bit so we thought we'd eat in the dining room at the end of the far wing of the house. Until this point, I'd had no reason to go to that end of the house. Imagine my surprise when I walked down the dark hall to set the table for dinner and found the hair on the back of my neck and arms go straight up. I also felt the usual tightness in my chest I get whenever there seems to be something else around. The presence was so strong and so dense that I stopped in my tracks. It gave off the energy or picture of a large, dark ugly toad, just squatting there, heavy and unhappy. I pushed forward, plunked the silverware and plates down on the table, and went to talk to Stephanie, who was helping my wife in the kitchen.

"So, your room, what the heck?" I began.

"I know, it's awful and I can't figure out why I don't like it down there, but I really, really don't."

"Yeah," I said, "I think you should probably switch ends of the house."

So that's what Stephanie did. She took one of the other rooms in our end the house. That night we heard the same thumps and bumps we'd heard the first night, but now we noticed they were all at the other end of the house. At least twice I heard a door close down there and Stephanie, who had managed to get a better night's sleep, told me in the morning that she'd heard the doors closing as well.

I couldn't get the strangeness out of my head. As Sunday dawned, I ventured back into that side of the house and went into the room vacated by Stephanie. The last thing I wanted to do was open myself to this creature, whatever it was, but I relaxed a little and focused on it some more.

If it hadn't been so sad, it would have been comical. The far wing of the house was the one that was most affected, but I was pretty sure the presence used to affect the entire lake house. In the 1940s, the property belonged to an old man. He lived there fulltime and never intended it as a holiday home. He had built his house, all two rooms of it, out by the lake to get away from people. His greatest desire was to be left alone; he'd picked an isolated spot near the water so he could have the solitude he wanted most. The only trouble was that after the Second World War, people began doing things like building holiday homes, and the old man quickly found himself surrounded by people, lots of happy, holidaying, friendly, outgoing, neighbourly people. He hated it. He hated them. I got all of this so quickly and so suddenly that it was like he was standing beside me, personally putting it into my head. It made sense, though; I could picture him sitting in his house, glaring out at everyone and never saying a word, but if they stepped on his property, watch out.

All in all, he wasn't the evil presence I had first intuited. Rather, he was like the Oscar the Grouch of ghosts. I guess when his house was torn down and the new one built, he hadn't bothered to move on. After all, as far as he was concerned, it was his home and no one else had the right to be there.

I asked Stephanie how she felt in the room and she told me she just felt uncomfortable.

"I know that. You mentioned that, but what else?" I pressed.

She thought about it a little more and then responded, "I guess I'd have to say, unwelcome, like I was being prodded all night until I left."

I actually smiled.

"What are you so happy about? That's not a good thing!" Stephanie said.

"I'm smiling because that matches up with everything I thought I was getting on this place."

I filled Stephanie in on who or what her roommate had been that night and she agreed that it made sense. She was also very happy to hear that he had no interest in going into the rest of the house as we had planned to stay until Monday morning.

That night, everyone bedded down, much as we had the night before. While we still heard bumps and the odd door closing in the other part of the house, it didn't bother us nearly as much, as we knew who was doing it, and we knew he wasn't planning to visit us. As we left the house, we avoided going into that wing, gathered our belongings, and made sure everything was spic and span for the next people coming in. Let's hope they had a less interesting time than we did.

While I never spoke to the guests who stayed in the house after us, I did ask our friends about the original property. They hadn't built the house, but they had seen pictures of the original structure. It was a small two-room cottage in about the same place as the far wing of the current house. I wasn't surprised, but it was nice to have it confirmed. I don't go around announcing to people that something not quite alive is in their home unless they ask me what I think. Many people don't know I pick up on stuff, so wouldn't ask. I never told our friends about the resident with whom they share their holiday home, but they never mentioned anything about it to me, so perhaps he doesn't mind them as much. We never did go back, although we were invited. I would say, if pressed, that we just didn't find the place very welcoming.

HATLEY CASTLE

IT SEEMS TO me that these "castles" built by rich men of industry carry some kind of curse. For example, coal baron Robert Dunsmuir never got to live in his monumental home, Craigdarroch Castle, as he died before it was completed. The curse seemed to follow his son, James, when he built Hatley Castle.

The Dunsmuir family was complicated, fractious, and messy. There is no shortage of literature about the family and their troubles. Alcoholism, litigation, and delusions of grandeur (one family member spent millions producing Hollywood movies, which she also starred in, in hopes of becoming famous—it didn't work) are just some of the follies this family suffered, not to mention losing their wealth in one generation. The Dunsmuirs were nothing if not interesting.

While all of the former Dunsmuir residences still house some of their deceased residents, Hatley Castle in particular hosts more than the usual share of energy and entities. I have encountered one of them myself, and it was pretty powerful and pretty annoyed. It was a she actually, but more on that later.

In 1906, James and Laura Dunsmuir purchased the property that would be home to Hatley Castle. At the time, James was British Columbia's Lieutenant Governor. The forty-room castle was built between 1908 and 1909, and exotic gardens were created— the lifestyle of the ultra-rich was on full display. Buildings were added over the years to make the estate closer to James's vision of a completely self-sustaining enterprise. Massive stables were built; there were multiple houses for staff, and the park even had it's own Chinatown for the garden workers—there were over one hundred men whose sole job it was to tend the gardens.

However, life was not perfect. In 1915, James and Laura lost their twenty-one-year-old son, James Jr. He went down on the ship *Lusitania* as he headed to England to join the war. His mother never recovered from the loss. James and Laura had hoped James Jr. would take over the family business, as his brother, Robert, was more interested in drinking and running around than working, and his sisters were characterized as "a wild lot, with money to burn." James Sr.'s brother, Alexander, had died from alcoholism in 1900 and James had been entrenched in a legal battle with his mother for years over who controlled the family business. There was no one else fit to be heir.

By 1939, both James and Laura were gone. Their children were either dead themselves or using up the family fortune much faster than it could be replenished. Combine this with the fact that Canada was just about to emerge from the Depression and join the Second World War, and the remaining Dunsmuirs suddenly realized they couldn't afford to keep Hatley Park any longer. In 1940, the heirs sold it to the Canadian Government for only 75,000 dollars. James had spent that same sum alone building a stone wall at the front of the property.

The government converted Hatley Park into a military college and Royal Roads was born. It remained a college from 1940 to 1990. During those decades, there were a number of additions to the buildings already on the grounds. In 1995, it was granted full status as a degree conferring university, and kept the name Royal Roads.

As soon as students started living at the castle, the stories started. For the first four years, until additional buildings were completed in 1944, the castle served as dorms for the students; this included James Jr.'s childhood bedroom. Students recounted stories of an old woman who would come in to James Jr.'s former room, which housed several young recruits. She would lift the sheet to peer at the bed's occupant. When she discovered it was not who she was looking for, she would grab the young man by the leg and drag him to the floor. In other rooms, students would complain of feeling a very cold hand on their shoulder when they were working late at night. It was as if the presence was urging them to go to bed. The ghostly presence was thought to be Laura Dunsmuir, but it was unclear whether she was displeased that someone else was in her beloved son's old room, or if she was trying to prevent them from going to war as her son had done, to protect them.

The other unpleasant spirit, the one I ran into, was that of Laura's personal maid, who had been carrying on a bit of a dalliance with a young sailor from the United States. James Sr. had his personal yacht, the *Dolaura*, anchored in the lagoon at the bottom of the castle's grounds and kept a substantial crew to run it. The yacht was over two hundred feet long, had a dining room that could seat twenty-four people, and the Dunsmuirs' personal suite had a large sitting area and a walk-in closet; the bedroom and bathroom in their suite was tiled and had sterling silver fittings. This was no simple pleasure boat. It would not have been unusual for a personal maid to accompany her mistress aboard the ship, and it would not have been difficult for this young woman to find some alone time with a young sailor. Their relationship blossomed and this rather innocent young woman fully believed she had found true love and behaved accordingly. When she discovered that she was pregnant, she told her lover that now they would be man and wife. The sailor, who was from Port Angeles, then broke the news to her that he already had a wife. The young woman, broken by the shame of being pregnant out of wedlock, threw herself from the third floor window of Hatley Castle to the patio below, dying as soon as her head struck the flagstones.

When I finished my degree at Royal Roads University, I was brought on as associate faculty for a few semesters to help ease new students into online learning. This meant that I had to attend the wine and cheese receptions to welcome students to their in-house portion of learning. These receptions were held in the castle itself. The lower level is often used for receptions of many kinds, but the upper levels of the castle, which house the former bedrooms and private chambers, are now used as offices for the university administration. On one occasion, I had gotten to the reception early and the catering staff was hurrying about so I took the opportunity to wander at will.

I made my way across the ground floor to the grand central staircase and headed up. I got to the top of the stairs, took three steps down the main corridor, and stopped. I felt like someone was standing in front of me, physically stopping me. Not only that, but the presence was angry. My overwhelming sense was that this was the young maid. Unsurprisingly, she's not a huge fan of men in general. She deeply resented me being there in what she felt was her space. I turned on my heel and headed downstairs (ever the brave adventurer that I am).

At one time, it was understood that no one was required to work in those offices by themselves because the feelings were so strong in this place. One investigator, Ed, told me that he'd been at the castle for an event and had also gone upstairs. He began walking down the hallway and heard someone coughing and heels clicking on tile floor. As he moved to the end of the hall, he realized the noises were coming from a bathroom there. He opened the door, but the bathroom was empty. There was no one else on the floor with him.

I've heard many tales of hauntings at Hatley Castle. Even people with low sensitivity to the spiritual feel uncomfortable there, and I know the university tries to downplay the stories. However, two people who have worked there have separately corroborated the stories.

I rarely hear any stories about strange encounters on the grounds of the park itself, which I find intriguing. If you park outside the gym and walk away from the castle, going past a building on your left and a small house on your right, you'll come to a walking trail. The first part of the trail before you turn toward the sea is one I have always found profoundly spiritual. I'm not sure what took place there, perhaps it was a sacred First Nations site, perhaps the energy comes from something more New Age, but there is something stirring in those woods. I'm not sure I'd feel comfortable walking through them alone, even during the daytime. It's not necessarily evil, but it is powerful and unpredictable.

The grounds of Hatley Castle are extensive and going out to the castle is quite the experience. They do give tours and the Japanese garden there rivals the one at the Butchart Gardens. If you visit the park, take notice of what you might sense. You will be amazed by the architecture and landscape, but you may be more even amazed at how many people still linger within its walls.

FORT RODD HILL AND
FISGARD LIGHTHOUSE
NATIONAL HISTORIC SITES

ANOTHER HAUNTED AND beautiful public spot to visit around Victoria is Fort Rodd Hill and Fisgard Lighthouse National Park. I have been to this location a number of times and it is pretty amazing. Though perched adjacent to one another on the coast—the lighthouse is a bit of a walk past the fort, on its own peninsula—these two sites are separate entities in terms of history and even hauntings. Luckily, you can explore both the upper and lower batteries of the fort, and the lighthouse keeper's house and the bottom of the tower to the lighthouse.

Fort Rodd Hill was established before British Columbia was even part of Canada. The British Navy began using the Esquimalt harbour for water and lumber between 1840 and 1855, and even set up three hospital huts. The need for something a little more permanent came during the Fraser River Gold Rush in 1858. The Americans and the British even had an armed standoff at Fort Rodd Hill in 1859, which didn't get resolved until 1871.

The first permanent coastal defences were built in 1870. The first set of guns was installed in 1893. They built new and more defensible guns for the Second World War in 1944, which remained there until 1962, when the site was converted into a national historic site. The garrison never actually saw active combat, but a submarine appeared in the harbour one night during the Second World War. It surfaced, then submerged, and wasn't seen again. When the big guns were fired, which was very infrequently, they often caused the windows at the Fisgard Lighthouse, and even those in homes in Esquimalt village, to break.

The fort is a rich and varied place spiritually speaking. There are so many nooks and crannies to explore, many of them built into the hillside. There have been reports over the years of people feeling uncomfortable in different places in the fort, feeling watched or unwelcome. Some people have even reported seeing fleeting shapes or shadows out of the corners of their eyes in the dark rooms. Dawn Kirkham, a local medium, has been able to figure out who some of the entities are.

In the battlements, the room where you can watch video re-enactments of things that happened at the site, there is an angry man who committed suicide. Dawn and her team have tried to help him move on, but he doesn't feel like he can. He's tormented by what he did, and he also does not completely realize that he's deceased. If you sense him, you will feel like you are being watched and that you are not welcome.

In the barracks, there are a number of male spirits, but also a few females. Dawn has discovered that the women were most likely prostitutes brought in to keep the men happy in their isolated spot, but she is not sure why their spirits remain there. Perhaps the men got a bit rough and an accident claimed the women? Dawn can't say for sure, but their spirits are quite jovial, easy going, and positive.

In the officers' quarters, Dawn's team encountered something very unpleasant. Not only was the spirit angry and mean, but he wanted everyone out. Dawn would have loved to have had more time in there to see if she could figure out exactly what was going on, but the group energy dissipated the entity.

I have had similar experiences. If you are in a haunted location, it can be quite difficult to pinpoint what energy is actually spirit energy because everyone has an energy of their own. You will find this in day-to-day life: some people have a positive energy around them that brings you up while others have a negative energy that brings you down. This is a normal reaction to someone else's energy and it works the same way with spirits.

THE FISGARD LIGHTHOUSE is one of the most photogenic lighthouses in Canada. And it is as haunted as it is scenic.

Built in 1860, this lighthouse has a long history. Over the years it had twelve lighthouse keepers, and two of them died while taking care of the light. In 1950, the military built a causeway out to the lighthouse, not only to make it easier to access, but also as a military obstacle. But before then the only way to reach the lighthouse was by boat. The last lighthouse keeper to tend to the light before it went automatic was Josiah Gosse, who lived there until 1928.

The man who died in the most dramatic fashion while keeping the Fisgard Light was Joseph Dare. Joseph set off one morning to row over to the village of Esquimalt to pick up his mail. Something happened on the way there and Joseph fell out of the boat and drowned. Is it his energy that has remained in the home?

Lighthouse keeping was once perceived as a cushy job, and many thought the posts were given out as political favours by whatever government was in power at the time. The reality was that it was a very tough job. You never got a full night's sleep, you were isolated, and the pay was terrible. Furthermore, if you got sick, no one would know until it was too late. In order for it to spin round and round, the light was balanced in a mercury bath.

This bath had to be strained every month. At the time, no one knew what mercury did to a human body, so many of the lighthouse keepers either ended up with crippling arthritis or went completely insane. It was assumed that the keepers went insane because of the isolation, but it was far more likely due to the mercury. If a keeper wanted a helper, he could hire one, but the wages came out of his own meagre pay. The government provided scant rations. Any attempt to supplement these often ended poorly. One keeper saved every penny he could and bought a goat, a cow, and a few chickens. After a particularly nasty storm, he emerged to discover the animals had all been blown off the island. Some keepers attempted to grow vegetables, but the gardens were soon abandoned because the wind refused to allow anything to grow.

I have been to the lighthouse many times; it's one of my favourite places to visit on Vancouver Island. When I've been there, I've often been aware that I'm not alone. There has been more than one time when I've been the only person physically in the house, and I could have sworn someone was in there with me. I have heard noises on calm days: footsteps or doors closing even though there are no longer any doors to close. One time, I heard a man cough very close to me. Other people have experienced these things and more. One report included a handful of pebbles being tossed at the window; when the woman went out to look, no one was anywhere near the lighthouse. The woman remained in the house for some time, and it happened three more times. At that point, she got spooked and left. I have to admit, she lasted longer than I would have.

Dawn has picked up two distinct entities in the house. The first one was a very present, very strong male energy. Dawn would have been able to experience more, but unfortunately the group she was with spread the energy too much and she wasn't able to focus as well as she would have liked. She said that the man was strong, but not bad. The energy I've felt there has not been one that wanted me to leave, but one that was happy to have company. I'm sure all of the lighthouse keepers felt that way quite often.

The other energy that Dawn picked up was that of an "elemental." Elementals are a distinct type of spirit, often described as an elf, gnome, leprechaun, fairy, brownie, mermaid, or even goblin. The job of an elemental is to look after the natural kingdom and keep it sustained. If you notice yourself unwinding and relaxing in nature, that is believed to be the work of an elemental. The one Dawn picked up on was of a very primal, ancient being. Elementals are created by the land to protect it. This one was not overly bright or cunning; it was gentle and just happy to exist and do its job. Dawn said it was exceptionally strong near the fort and the lighthouse, which makes a lot of sense as both are embedded in nature.

If you have a chance, do head to Fort Rodd Hill and the Fisgard Lighthouse. If nothing else, you will get to see a small glimpse of what life was like for the men and some women who spent a great deal of time there. They have left more behind than a bunch of old buildings.

ACKNOWLEDGEMENTS

WRITING A BOOK is never a one-person endeavour—at least *this* one sure wasn't! I want to use up as little space as possible, but also want to make sure everyone who is so deserving of thanks receives it. Those of you who feel you deserve some thanks —and we both know you do—and were not mentioned by name, I apologize unreservedly. In light of my intentions, the following people need to be acknowledged:

Taryn Boyd, Tori Elliott, Renée Layberry, Kate Scallion, and Pete Kohut—and everyone at Touchwood—thank you for seeing this book before I did. You have made this experience an adventure I want to enjoy again.

Thanks for the author-to-author writing advice from Barbara Smith, Brennan Storr, and John Adams. You kept me focused and positive while you each imparted some very hard-won wisdom.

My Ghostly Walk friends, you are all amazing and I learn from each of you every time we work together. Thanks, Brynne, for letting me steal your jokes!

To all the wonderful people who shared their stories with me: I won't list names as some of you have asked me not to, but it's important that you get thanked. You know who you are, and I'm eternally grateful. Many people took time to meet with me and share of their hearts and experiences; I'm honoured by the gift you have given.

My kind coworkers, Alison, Corrina, and Kim: thank you so much for putting up with me while I relentlessly talked about this project.

Much gratitude to Andrea Bailey and Dawn Kirkham, who graciously and comfortably invited me into their ghost investigation worlds: you showed me that there is a compassionate side to working with the spirit world, and you are both excellent examples of that.

Thanks to Ray Shipka, who took so many pictures for this book. You are an artist, sir, and I'm grateful I was lucky enough to have you offer—and I'm happy I was smart enough to accept.

Thank *you*, reader and fellow ghost inquirer. I hope that your story and experiences will appear in the next book. Please feel free to contact me at ghoststoryguy@gmail.com.

And finally, to Jason: thank you.

PHOTO CREDITS

COVER PHOTO Hatley Castle, davemantel, istockphoto.com

AUTHOR PHOTO Gary Quinn

INTERIOR PHOTOS by Ray Shipka, except for the following:

    HOTEL ON LOCHSIDE DRIVE, P. 158 Fotogal, istockphoto.com

    THE WILKINSON JAIL, P. 166 Hallmark Heritage Society
    Archives

    HOME ON ELK LAKE DRIVE, P. 172 Luca Pierro, Stocksy United

    VICTORIA-AREA LAKE HOUSE, P. 178 Christian Tisdale,
    Stocksy United

IAN GIBBS was born in the United Kingdom and emigrated to Canada when he was young. As such, he carries with him the celtic beliefs and gifts of his heritage, and has always been fascinated by storytelling, ghosts, and hauntings. He lived in several city centres across Canada before settling in Victoria, arguably one of the most haunted places in all of Canada, in 2000. During the summer months, he guides tours for Victoria's popular Ghostly Walks walking tours. Visit GhostStoryGuy.com, and listen to his podcast, The Ghost Story Guys.